Animal Lovers' Bedside Stories

Sue Greenall

ACKNOWLEDGMENTS

—ɯ—

No matter how badly how your day has gone,
your pets always give you a second chance.

Edited by Kathy Callan-Rondeau & Helen K. Hopkins
Technical assistance by Dinah Rojek, Jo Steele
and Mary Ann Barcellona
Cover painting by Beth Carlson
(Habibi Bukharis, Girlfrien' & Nudge)
Illustrated by the pets

The Animal Lovers' Bedside Stories
Copyright 2010 by Susan Greenall
Second printing
All Rights Reserved

Printed in the United State of America
Printed by R.C. Brayshaw & Company, Inc
ISBN# 978-1-4276-4774-0

For additional copies
Greenall@vermontel.net
www.vermontel.com/~greenall

SHOW ME YOUR PET,
AND I WILL TELL YOU WHO YOU ARE....

Barn Friends - Beth Carlson
Aleser, Willie Wonka, Grilfrien', Nudge & Strubbles

Please consider adopting your next pet

Also by Sue Greenall

The Animal Lovers' Bedtime Reader

Reviews

We appreciate you granting permission for the use of your stories for assignments for our reading classes. They help raise the rigor in instruction and assessments. Hoke County Schools, SC

—ᵚᵚ—

Well written anecdotes of the escapades and antics of a bevy of fur and feathered creatures told by one with uncanny insight to animal behavior. This book should gladden the heart of any animal lover.
The Carriage Journal,

—ᵚᵚ—

The stories are addictive as is the author's love toward the animals who have touched her life. Woven amongst the tales are traces of heartwarming and sensible philosophy on animal relationships providing subtle counsel on ornery ponies, ferret escape artists, and house-goats.
The Morgan Horse Magazine,

—ᵚᵚ—

This is a cozy little book that will touch the hearts of pet lovers
Upper Valley Life Magazine

The Vermonters' Guide to Gathering, Growing & Cooking with Local Foods

I appreciate that the recipes are divided by food items, as localvore cooking involves building a meal around particular seasonal ingredients. This cookbook will certainly help you become a more successful localvore.

Caroline Abels - Editor, Vermont's Local Banquet

Animal Lovers' Bedside Stories

DANGLING BY A MODIFIER

The scratching at my feet was telling me that Mr. Magoo, my free-range ferret, was feeling frisky. He delighted in rolling on my feet and taking a little nip now and again. Gypsy Rose Lee had just jumped to the back of my chair, arching her feline back and purring in my ear and Meant To Be was circling in order to settle herself next to my desk for a doggy nap. I was never alone when I wrote this book.

I had the luxury of two windows by my computer that looked out onto the pastures where ten horses grazed. Seven had been the absolute limit, which we completely ignored, of horses to keep. If I was lucky, I could hear our thirty-one year old horse munching the grass on the lawn, as he knew no fence. At least once a year, someone would drive up our lane to tell us our horse was loose. He had been loose for fifteen years; such a person was new to the neighborhood.

Every day that was set aside for writing began with a slalom of tasks to be completed before I hit the keys. Feed the cats, give the ferret his treat, let out the dogs, feed the horses, play butt with the goat, check on the goose's swimming pool: I was maid service. But didn't these wonderful animals give me the reason to write? My horses carried me on countless adventures and introduced me to parts of the world I never would have seen otherwise. The cats and dogs and ferret and goat brought humor and laughter into my days.

Each story has its own origin. Some started as stories told in conversation. Some came to me based on a singular incident. Others were dictated by the animals themselves. I came to understand that I was giving them a voice as I wrote their stories. Some of the characters in this book are long past, but their spirit lives on in print. I am so blessed to have been included in so many adventures with animals and look forward to more.

Most challenging was formatting the book. Learning new software brings meaning to the phrase "user friendly." I had countless ice cream headaches having to remember that "place" meant "insert" and that the black arrow cursor did different things than the white arrow cursor. If the book were a painting, it would have over a million brush strokes!

I discovered that I had not paid much attention in eighth grade English class. I probably missed most of fifth, sixth and seventh grade too. I had no idea what subordinate clauses or dangling modifiers were. I could not recognize faulty parallelism and surely had not a clue what a qualifier was. My computer program coaxed me through hours and hours of reviewing my stories so that you, the reader, would not be upset should I split an infinitive.

My command of the English language was utterly shattered when it came to verbs; progressive tense, perfect tense, past perfect tense, past simple tense, future simple tense. All of this just made me tense. I dreamed up the idea of making a dartboard with all of the tenses. I could then throw a dart each time I was stumped and come up with an answer. Then there were the modal verbs, the countable and uncountable nouns and squinting modifiers. I would think that I would have remembered something called "squinting" when in eighth grade but apparently not.

I can only hope that the material is compelling enough for the reader to forgive my grammar. There are places where I did take liberties, after all, it is story telling.

Margaret & Mr. Magoo at play in my office

THE RIVER

The testing of the first submarine in the Passaic River in New Jersey was not the only historical event that ever happened there. It was also where I learned to swim with a horse.

I grew up in suburbia where trains took fathers off to New York City every morning and moms went to PTA meetings and helped with Girl Scouts. It did not take long to realize that I was not cut out to be a Girl Scout. All I ever wanted was a horse; living in suburbia was little help on that matter. Try as I did to convince my parents that the back patio would make a perfect barn, they did not buy it. Most painful was seeing other kids riding their horses alongside a road, with me pressing my face against the window of the car wishing for the entire world to be them. In suburbia, the only place to ride a horse was alongside a road or across someone's backyard. Amazingly, no one seemed to mind. Even the horse.

Armed with all of the knowledge one can glean from reading every horse book in the town library and watching every TV horse show, I knew everything I needed for one of my own. Flicka had taught me how to whistle for a horse, and Fury trained me to keep a sharp eye for things that scared horses and caused them to rear and paw in the air. Every TV cowboy demonstrated the kind of horsemanship I would need, including mounting and dismounting at a run. The Black Stallion assured me that it was safe to swim with a horse. I was so ready.

Long suffering was my mother. Every Wednesday afternoon, just before *My Friend Flicka* came on, she would drag my iron legged, wooden school desk down from my room on the second floor to place it in front of the TV in the living room. Once there, I would sling a dog leash over the top of the desk and mount it by placing my feet in the loops in the leash for stirrups. I had crayoned in a muzzle and ears and placed two blue polka dots for eyes on the left-hand side of the desk. It was a splendid mount. I still have that desk.

As far as I know, my father never knew about this. I doubt he would have noticed any resemblance of my desk to an equine. So it was the most surprising moment of my life when he gave me two hundred dollars to buy a horse on my thirteenth birthday. It was quite apparent that he didn't have the slightest idea what a horse cost, but then again, neither did I. Flicka and Fury came out of nowhere. I went horse shopping.

That first horse, to this day, remains the toughest, roughest, meanest animal I have ever known. My friend Linda can attest to that. One time, when Linda was feeding my horses for me, that mare chased her into a tree. Linda had to break off a branch and beat her way down and out of the paddock. But when you are thirteen, having begged for a horse all of your life, and are armed with the knowledge of those books from the library, you are not about to admit perhaps this horse was not the best choice.

Linda became my best friend because she also had a horse. Actually she rode a pony named Trigger who was a barrel of fun, but occasionally Linda snitched her sister's horse. Sunset was a whopping palomino mare who liked to kick out the side of the barn if not fed on time. We acquired some handy carpentry skills thanks to her. Linda and I would get home from school, race to the barn and meet each other at the old Cornish Farm. Perhaps the last piece of open land in New Jersey, it offered us great riding. However, we did have to negotiate suburbia to get there, I had to ride along a stretch of highly trafficked paved road and Linda had to cross the Erie Lackawanna train tracks, which ran right behind her house. We got to know that train schedule by heart.

I forgot to mention that the two hundred dollars did not stretch far enough to buy any equipment for my horse. I had an old belt for a bridle, borrowed a bit, and I rode bareback. My collection of bruises from getting dumped finally produced a saddle for Christmas, but by then I was a pretty darn good bareback rider. Plus it was warmer in the winter.

It never occurred to Linda or me that we should not have been doing the things we did. We would hang ice skates over our horses necks, ride three to four miles to a frozen swamp, and go skating. For

some reason, the horses remained tied to their trees until we came back. We hooked a toboggan behind Trigger, and drove him over the tracks and through the Cornish Farm at a gallop. Sometimes Linda would fall off, and I would be left in the back of the toboggan grabbing for the reins. When Linda managed to get Sunset from her sister, that high-powered mare would start to buck, and Linda would half dismount, lying across the saddle with one leg in the stirrup, the other one flailing in the air, before getting her back in control.

But, it was our adventures in the Passaic River that we still talk about. Winding slowly through our town the water was never anything but brown. I later learned that was pollution, but we attributed it to mud. There was plenty of mud in our part of New Jersey and I challenge any place in the United States to top it. Located just outside what is now known as The Great Swamp, it was just that: a swamp. And the Passaic River was part of that.

Linda and I had a trail along the river which we used when the river wasn't flooded, which was rare. Any rainfall event pumped up the river, some actually causing flooding over the roadway and bridge. Because of that, the bridge was an open metal grid. When cars hit it, it made an impressive, rrrrump, rrrrump, rrrrump, sound. And we rode our horses over that bridge. My horse and Trigger never seemed to mind the bridge, but Sunset had to be ridden backwards over it. One of us would stand at the curve to warn of any cars approaching while Linda or her sister would twirl Sunset around and back her over.

We rode over the bridge to attain the only bank where we could access the river to go swimming. Vegetation, steepness or someone's backyard kept us from any other location. But just upstream of the bridge was a low bank that offered an ideal spot to get ourselves wet. Of course, we rode bareback and barefoot.

Getting into the river tested our skills and determination as riders. None of the horses thought it was a good idea as that bank was slippery. What helped us was the constant state of flooding; it hid the real bank enough so that the horse would simply fall in. Once in, we would grasp their manes and float above them as they surged up and down in the water as they turned and swam back to the safety of the bank. On occasion, one of us would part with our horse and have to swim like crazy to get to the bank before him.

It was a good thing that we didn't know that not all horses can swim; it would have spoiled the best memories we have of being kids with horses.

HAVE YOU SEEN THE FERRET?

The furniture in our house was arranged for the inconvenience of the ferret. The living room love seat was just far away enough from the plant table to deter the leap which could bring the ferret to the number-one–favorite-pastime of all weasels; digging in dirt. The DNA which programs weasels to dig burrows into the ground, has been lying dorment for several hundred generations since captivity and it can't wait to get out. Domestic ferrets do not even know what dirt is until they see it, then their DNA clicks into action and they start digging to China. It is bad, very bad, for houseplants.

The footstool for the chair by the television in the kitchen is another piece of furniture that must be arranged carefully. Should it serve access to the chair, and should the chair be pushed back just a tad too close to the countertop, there would arrive a ferret. First order of business would be the sink and some serious head poking into the garbage disposal. Once his feet were wet, the window plants would get the same treatment as the ones in the living room, only this time the little paws would be wet from the sink and would track teeny weensy footprints all over the counter; a form of sponge painting with mud. The stove would suffer the same fate. Given enough time, the liquid soap dispenser would be toppled to just the right angle to allow it to drip; adding a sticky element to the sponge painting.

The lower kitchen cabinets had rubber bands on the knobs to hold them shut in order to protect the contents from being rummaged through by a ferret. Slinky as he was, he never broke anything, but then there was the one occasion where he accidentally dumped the cleanser container and tracked that throughout the dishes. People have commented on how clean my kitchen is but it was never my intention, rather the after effect of cleaning up after a ferret foray.

The ferret would be long gone before our discovery of his adventures; good thing for him. On the rare occasion when caught in the act, his innocent little eyes would announce that, after all, he was a ferret; what did we expect? I would grab him, get right into his face and scold "bad ferret", and he would just smother me with kisses. Discipline was lost with ferrets. We were also reminded that the *Ferrets Make Excellent Pets* handbook, which we only refer to when having a ferret crisis, clearly stated, "Ferrets should not be given free run of

the household as they can easily get into trouble." Too late for us; the ferret was already loose, and there was no going back.

The hours of après ferret frolic clean-up trained both myself and the husband to carefully eye measure the distances of the house furniture whenever we passed through a room.

One of our morning rituals was to ask, "Have you seen Mr. Magoo?" Since he had the run of the house, the answer was not always easy. Sometimes he would disappear for day-long naps, and only appear like a ghost running down the hallway for a quick drink before returning to his nap. Napping, for ferrets, is a way of life.

It was possible to keep track of him by sound. Ferret sneezes are half the volume of a kitty sneeze and can give up the most concealed of locations. There was also the pitter-patter of little ferret feet that, amazingly, were not as light footed as one would think. Scurrying across a rug produced a hurried, shuffling noise distinct to weasels. One would wonder what was thumping down the staircase until one caught him in the act.

Since ferrets often travel at speed, darting back and forth across a room in order to slither under every piece of furniture on the way to a destination, one was more likely to hear, not see, a moving ferret. Glimpses might be had, rather like watching a Monty Python skit occurring in our own home.

Keeping tabs on the ferret was useful information for situations that one would never be able to predict. We learned this the hard way. Shortly after we acquired our ferret, the husband left to officiate at a horse show in Ohio, and I could not locate Mr. Magoo. I checked the bottom of the laundry hamper, his little cardboard box in the corner of the closet (a house of sorts), his spot behind the television where the VCR made for a pleasant, warm napsite and his side of the husband's armoire. The last site was rather new. The husband, somewhat tired of sharing the closet with a ferret, installed an armoire in the bedroom; the thought being that since it had doors, it would be ferret proof. I considered it a compliment and sign of affection in that the ferret moved into the armoire along with the husband's clothes.

Still, I could find no ferret. I checked the china cupboard (which he opened by lying on his back and kicking his feet), the family heirloom armoire in the living room where a hole in its floor - cut by the husband's great aunt for some unfathomable reason - offered ferret access, and the pantry where I kept grocery bags. Nothing.

I felt a little panic trickle through me. Doing a mental checklist of when Mr. Magoo was last accounted for, I realized that it was prior to the husband's departure. The husband was a progressive packer when he planned a trip. Two days before he was to leave, out would come the suitcase, and he would add items with intermittent care until he felt he had everything that he would need. The suitcase would lie on a low bench by the window, and often contained a cat, or two, as it offered a warm and comfy view of the bird feeder. It could also offer a warm and comfy napsite for a ferret.

The husband never would have noticed a napping ferret while zipping up his suitcase, and the ferret never would have noticed he was bouncing down a luggage belt into the belly of a seven-forty-seven jet; serious nappers that ferrets are. I had heard about a dog that went missing in a jet for over a month before he was found. A ferret could go missing for years! My fear that Mr. Magoo was circling Chicago sent me rampantly leaving phone messages informing every possible person with whom the husband might connect that he should check his luggage immediately upon arrival. Imagine the reaction of a horse show manager when I explained that perhaps a ferret was coming to his show office!

The husband called the moment he got the message. Knowing the ways of ferrets only too well, he had opened his luggage in the security of a bathroom and rummaged through it for a napping ferret. Nothing. He said he was ever so relieved. Then the thought occurred to him that perhaps the ferret had escaped the luggage, slinky as he was, and was on a flight to California at that very moment.

"Relax," I said, when he phoned me quite in dread, "I found him." I was not sure if the long sigh at the other end of the line was relief, or the sound of a man who could not understand how his life had come to be run by a ferret.

The ferret had been discovered shortly after my last phone call. The cats, usually bound to my legs, were peering up the stairwell to the closed door at the top. A tiny white snout was peering back. Apparently Mr. Magoo had followed the husband up to the second floor when the suitcase was retrieved and had settled in for a two day nap before noticing anything was wrong. He greeted me with a "where have you been?" look, then trundled down the stairs for a bite to eat before settling into another nap who knows where.

From that point on, we kept better track of the ferret.

Houseguests, upon arrival, were forewarned about leaving their luggage, bags or purses on the floor unless they wanted to take home a ferret. That was usually enough to make them exceedingly fastidious with their belongings. We also came to realize that not everyone thought a marauding white weasel was cute, so,  when the guest list was made up people were characterized as "Ferret" or "No Ferret" visitors. We had no wish to give anyone a heart attack as they pulled the covers back on their bed only to find that they were not alone.

"No Ferret" visitors became a concern should we fail to find the ferret in time, which had happened more than once. One particularly adamant "No Ferret" guest went to bed not knowing that we had not located Mr. Magoo.

"You know where he is, right?" she asked timidly.

"Don't worry," I replied, avoiding the look from the husband. "But perhaps you should shut your bedroom door."

"He can't get under the door can he?" she gasped.

"Only his snout," I said, trying to lighten things up. Another look from the husband.

Dreading the thought that Mr. Magoo had somehow managed to get into the guest bedroom, in which case, he was now locked IN with the "No Ferret" guest, we scoured the house for him. About two in the morning, we found him sleeping in a plastic cooler in the pantry. The rationale of such a spot eluded me entirely, but I was ever so grateful to see his little face.

Service people also became a concern. In and out of the house they would go as they needed tools and parts from their truck. Alert as they promised to be, a ferret could easily slither out the door without them noticing. A "close door quickly – Ferret loose" sign was affixed to all of our doors, but we still were uneasy to have strangers in the house with Mr. Magoo afoot.

The morning the telephone repair crew was due I locked Mr. Magoo safely in the bedroom. Our telephones had been acting up; buzzing, scratchy noises, and irritating clicks. Two amiable Vermont Telephone repairmen, armed with meters and probes, arrived to determine the problem.

The husband, never wanting to miss anything, had phones everywhere: the barn, the shop, the carriage house, the basement, the upstairs guest room, the office, the kitchen and the bedroom. The repairmen were fairly confident that the problem was one of the outside phones that had corroded wires due to their exposure. It never occurred to us that, upon not finding the cause, they would let themselves into the house. Remember, this was Vermont.

I was in front of the house, the husband in the shop, when we heard the blood-curdling scream. It sounded just like something out of Alfred Hitchcock followed by uncontrollable laughter that turned into a somewhat heated conversation between our two amiable repairmen. Running to the house, we discovered the noise coming from the bedroom. Uh, oh.

Apparently, the cause of the phone problem was the bedside jack. Lying on the floor, under the bed, face up, the somewhat portly repairman had been busily testing the wires when Mr. Magoo ran over his face; blood curdling scream. The second repairman, witnessing the event, thought his partner's reaction funny; uncontrollable laughter. The first repairman did not think it was funny at all; heated conversation. We arrived just in time to calm things down and explain that Mr. Magoo was not a large rodent, rather a very domesticated weasel. A few ferret kisses later the repairman agreed it was pretty funny, and could not wait to tell his wife. I am not sure she believed him.

BE DAZZLED

"**D**addy, Mom, I just have to have this horse," gasped Charlotte as they greeted her on Parents' Day at camp. "He is just the most wonderful horse in the world, and I can train him to be a champion, I just know it. Please, come see him. His name is Dazzle!"

Charlotte's were not the first parents to be dragged by their little girl to view a horse that seemed like nothing special to them, but was everything to her. However, in Charlotte's case, she had thirty something horses at home, some quite fancy, so the attraction to this somewhat average looking pinto gelding befuddled them. "Smile," the mother said to her husband, "she'll get over it."

Two weeks later they received a phone call. It was from the farm that leased Dazzle to the summer camp. It was short and to the point. "Thank you for your letter offering to buy Dazzle, but our policy is not to sell horses under contract to camps. Should you wish to pursue this after camp is over, we would be happy to speak with you."

"Did she offer to buy this horse?" gasped the father, who knew darn well that they did not need any more horses, none, especially this one.

"I'll talk with her," steadied the mother, wondering how her imaginative twelve year old daughter had not only found where the horse came from, but had managed to get out a letter from a camp that did not allow such things.

At the end of camp session, Charlotte reluctantly left Dazzle to go home. She heard the lecture about obeying camp rules, and how she could have gotten into trouble, and all about respecting her parents' decisions. She said nothing, but put up photos of Dazzle on her bedroom wall and waited patiently for summer to end.

"Camp is over," she announced one day in late August. Not understanding, her parents just nodded. "Can I call them?"

"Call who?"

"You know, the farm, the farm where Dazzle lives."

Her parents were dumbfounded that their daughter, with a barn of carefully selected horses, still yearned for the somewhat average pinto gelding. So much for her getting over it! So much for her understanding of why they had the horses they did. Now what?

"We don't need another horse, dear," was the answer.

"He's not just another horse, he is special; please, can we just go see?" she begged.

"Honey, the horse lives in Vermont, we live in Florida!" answered the father hoping that his daughter would see this logic.

"Please?"

Since Charlotte was about to launch into her teen years, her parents were unsure as to the next step. She was old enough not to be treated like a child, yet still without the wisdom she would need for such decisions. Not wanting to shut her down altogether, they struggled for a solution. I was it. Basically because I lived in Vermont.

"How would you like to go look at a horse for us," they asked over the phone, after which they briefly outlined the situation. "We want you to find something wrong with the horse, which should not be too hard, so we can give our daughter a reason why we are not buying him." When I learned where the horse lived, I hesitated. Yes, I knew the place. Yes, I knew the owner. I already knew this was not going to be so simple.

"Hi there," I said over the phone, "I would like to set up an appointment to see a camp horse named Dazzle."

"We have several hundred horses here," the nice lady on the phone answered patiently. "Which camp, description and why do you want to see him."

"Kamp Kemmerer, chestnut pinto gelding and we are interested in buying him."

"Hmm, let me check." After a bit, she came back to the phone, "Well, we have a lot of pinto geldings, but we don't have a Dazzle, are you sure?"

I was not expecting that answer, but further descriptions and questions got me nowhere. I was just about ready to concede defeat when I asked if, perhaps, I could have a look at the chestnut pinto geldings.

"Sure, what are you looking for?"

"Just a nice family horse," I said, "I'll know it when I see it."

"Fine, come up on Tuesday, it's our slow day."

My report to the family was met with disappointment by Charlotte, and hopeful anticipation by her parents that the Dazzle situation would soon be over. Determined, Charlotte sent me pictures of her dream horse and made me promise that I would take the time to look for him. "Perhaps they forgot his name", she said with the eternal optimism of youth.

I gathered two friends to accompany me on the trip an hour north of where I lived. We had lunch and worked out a strategy; both of them delighted at the thought of espionage to find a horse. While I would talk to the owner, they would covertly scout out the horses looking for Dazzle. They had the photos; how hard could it be?

We were unprepared for the corral full of horses brought together for our behalf. If there were a hundred, half were pintos. From here to forever stretched out an assortment of blacks and bays, and chestnuts, an Appaloosa or two, but predominantly pintos. "Wow," my friends whispered, "this is going to be harder than we thought!"

Proper protocol, when buying a horse, is to shoot the breeze about everything and anything about horses as long as it is not about the horse in question. Like a couple of farmers discussing the crops, I mentioned friends who had purchased horses from his stable, told stories about how well they did, he told me about buying horses out West, the rising cost of feed, and how making a living with horses was no easy life. We were sizing each other up for the eventual negotiations on price, something we may or may not come to, but important should it come to pass. I was letting him know that I knew enough influential people that he had best be honest with me, and he was letting me know that he knew the market as well as I did and that he expected fair trade.

His back was to the corral, so only I could see my friends frantically searching for Charlotte's Dazzle. I could see them point to a horse, peer at the pictures, shake a head and move on to the next one. Periodic glances sent my way were a clear message, "Keep him talking!"

"Can't help you with names," explained the owner over the Dazzle question, "the camps give them those. We have too many horses here for names; they just have numbers. That Dazzle horse could be any of these, or he could be leased out or sold."

As he spoke, I could see my young friend bobbing along the fence line and then stop. I saw her peer into her coat at the pictures, look up, peer again and then start gesturing in my direction. There, at the gate, stood Dazzle!

A hundred horses. No name. No way to find him and he found us!

I kept my composure, although not easily, as my friends were jumping up and down in glee, hardly keeping to the plan of horse espionage. I turned the subject to the task at hand, and the owner and I worked out several horses that might suit my needs. "I had a customer", I said, "who liked pintos, and I was to select one suitable for them." I did everything I could not to show any preference for Dazzle.

Of all things, the three horses out of those hundred the owner selected, the first was Dazzle! Perhaps because he was standing by the gate? Or perhaps it was just fate. That horse walked by me with a look in his eye, which made me feel like a pawn in a scheme dreamed up by a twelve-year-old girl and a chestnut pinto gelding. I felt a bit used. I could not fault the horse when I tried him. He was green but willing. He offered me a comfortable ride and never made a wrong move. I could hardly say the same for the other two. The parents would not be so happy with this report, but Dazzle held me to tell the truth; which I did.

"Sorry," I said, "I could not fault him," when I called the parents. I could hear Charlotte's shouts of glee in the background. "Of course, he is not in the caliber of your horses, but that doesn't make him a horse without value. However, he would have to pass the vet and no guarantees there." Still determined to find an end to Dazzle, the parents instructed me to find the toughest vet in Vermont to do the exam.

Dazzle passed.

This was not going well for the parents. Charlotte remained determined. The only thing that now stood between her and her dream horse was price, something a twelve-year-old girl has little understanding of.

Here's the rub about going to a horse dealer and buying a horse. The value has nothing to do with the horse, and everything to do with how much you want it. Horse dealers are genetically adept at sensing "want" and know how to put a value on it. I was not sure if the owner realized this was the Dazzle about whom he had received a letter from the camp or if he was just driving a hard deal as the price was twice what he was worth.

Her parents decided that this horse could be a valuable lesson for Charlotte. She would have to pay the amount over his fair market worth, and at age twelve, that amount was inconceivable. It was more than birthday money, more than a year's allowance, more than anything she could possibly earn. Dazzle was about to test her more than anything in her life.

I was quick to point out that there was a lesson built into all of this, a lesson that could serve Charlotte well in her lifetime. It was time for her to learn the ways of horse dealing and the basics of negotiation. The prize was Dazzle, and we would soon learn, including Charlotte, what he was truly worth.

No negotiations were to happen before Charlotte agreed to a contract with her parents about payment. They would loan her the money and expect timed payments with a deadline for final payment. The deal had to be complete before she could take possession of the horse. The purchase price would be the result of Charlotte's negotiations with the owner. It was perhaps the first time in her life that she realized that one does not necessarily lay down the asking price when buying a horse. She was in new territory and knew it.

Dazzle was leased from the stable and boarded near our farm. After a month, under my direction, Charlotte contacted the owner and discussed price. She did an admirable job explaining the reasons why she felt he was worth less and ended by giving her offer, half. Of course, it was turned down. "Round one," I said, "good job." I was not so sure she agreed with this game of cat and mouse after being turned down. She was seeing this as a no win situation. If she paid the full price she would be working him off for a long, long time; or she lost the horse. She was feeling some purchase pain, just what her parents had hoped for.

What they did not expect was her rebound of determination and innovative methods of finding that money. One morning I received a call from her mother.

"I just want you to know what you have gotten us into," she quipped.

Me? This was not my idea...

"This morning I found my daughter going through my jewelry box picking out gold pieces. Seems she saw an ad on television, "cash for gold," and she is stripping the place!"

I had to stifle the chuckle. Charlotte was being resourceful!

Next was a letter to friends and relatives explaining that for Christmas Charlotte would be accepting cash instead of presents, in order to purchase Dazzle. It was called "The Dazzle Fund" and she would supply each donor with an autographed picture of herself and the special horse.

With her resources calculated, Charlotte had a pretty clear idea of how long she would be paying off this horse depending on the final price. Full price meant two Christmas's, a birthday and a long summer of extra chores; anything less was a life less encumbered. Negotiation took on a new meaning for her, and she was ready.

At the end of two months on the lease, Charlotte placed another call. "Yes, she liked the horse. Yes, he was doing well. However," she cleared her throat, "I am only twelve and will be paying for this horse myself. He still needs a lot of training and, while he might be worth this price eventually, he is not right now. He needs more training. I will offer you fifteen hundred dollars less than what you are asking. Otherwise, you can take him home and pay to winter him, and he probably won't bring that price again until next summer."

Charlotte waited with a dry mouth for the response. She had rolled the dice, with Dazzle on the line, and the panic inside her was building as she waited to learn the fate of not only her future Christmas's, but of the horse that had started all this.

"Really," she gasped, "it's a deal?" She just about squealed with delight, but remembering herself as a future businesswoman, she cleared her throat and said, "I will have the check in the mail today."

I gave her a big hug, turned and gave that somewhat average chestnut pinto gelding a big hug and grinned at the thought of the horse dealer who had grasped the situation and did the right thing. I would do business with him again, in a heartbeat.

Buoyed by the thought of calling Dazzle her own, plus having done some quick mental calculation that one Christmas, half a birthday, and only part of her summer would pay him off, Charlotte took the horse from his stall and led him out of the barn for some nice grass. He was hers, only hers, and he was no longer average, he was well above average.

Dazzle never let us down. He did not aspire to great things for, in truth, he was just average. But he never went wrong, always had a good attitude, and remained Charlotte's "special" horse even when she had some very above average horses at her disposal.

What were the odds, I thought, that he would have been standing at that gate at the only opportunity he would ever have to improve on his life. How did he know?

KING SOLOMON'S RING

Swimming elegantly on my neighbor's pond were two bachelor Chinese ganders, Willie and Waylon, short for Willie Nelson and Waylon Jennings. They bore no resemblance to their country singer namesakes other than they liked to hear themselves sing. Every night my neighbor called them from the pond to the safety of the cow barn. The two would waddle along, singing their way home; sometimes a harmony, sometimes a lively jingle. Their voices carried over the valley to us; a reassurance that day was done.

The pond was spacious and surrounded on one side by woods, the other by the cow pastures. Willie and Waylon were no dummies; they knew that they were not alone out there. There were foxes, fisher cats and coyotes lurking in the woods, and barred owls, red tail hawks and bald eagles in the air. They watched each other's backs, spending the day in the water where they were safest. A large submerged rock served as a perfect parking place, giving on-lookers the impression that they were walking on water, their secret revealed only when the water level dropped in the late summer.

One quick flash of movement, when Willie was not looking, took him. We all heard Waylon's honk of alarm, but it was too late. Waylon steadfastly refused to leave the pond, and his rock, for the safety of the barn at night from that point forward. He would swim around all day, and stand on his rock all night. Waylon was now alone. Or so we thought.

Every pond in Vermont gets scrutinized by every migrating duck, goose, or merganser in the spring. The snow is barely melting when the quacking, honking, and wing flapping birds swoop down for a looksee. The courtship, the nesting, the raising of a new generation, occurs in a few short, but busy, months before they flap off again, leaving their fledglings to figure things out on their own. Waylon's pond was no exception.

The pair of Mallard ducks on the pond that year had raised an impressive brood of six ducklings. Their progress from fuzzy striped balls that bobbed in the water, to a string of obedient ducklings driving a V in the water as they kept up with their mother, to young adults, was all done in Waylon's little kingdom. He kept his distance, curious, but respectful. His "honking" meant nothing to birds that spoke "quack", but he sang nevertheless. He sang for no apparent reason other than he liked his own voice.

The shorter days of early autumn call ducks to take flight for their long trip to warmer lands. The parents left first. Confused, and surely feeling lonely, the six young ducks paddled out to Waylon's submerged rock and spent the night with him. By morning, they were paddling along behind him, driving a V through the water, with apparently no concern that their guide was not of their kind.

Konrad Lorenz is perhaps the most referenced naturalist when it comes to animal behavior. He was a Nobel-Prize winning zoologist who studied animals both in the wild and in his home, in pre-World War II Austria. Lorenz experimented with imprinting at birth and learned that newly hatched Mallard's would accept him as "mother" if he quacked at them the moment they hatched. They would obediently waddle after him in a tightly huddled formation just as ducklings follow their mother. However, he quickly learned that the mother figure must not exceed a certain height, for, should he stand up, the ducklings would scatter in confusion. This led to his leading them about in a squatting position, quacking continuously, in order to keep his little flock happy. One Sunday, a group of passing tourists, unable to see the ducklings in the high grass, thought him quite peculiar!

Lorenz wrote about his animal adventures and theories in his book, *King Solomon's Ring*, called such after the legend of a magic ring that allowed King Solomon, son of David, to speak with animals. "Our fellow creatures can tell us the most beautiful stories," wrote Lorenz, "because the truth about nature is always far more beautiful even than what our great poets sing of it."

Neither Waylon, nor the ducks, seemed to be taking Konrad Lorenz's work seriously. Waylon honked; the ducks quacked. Waylon was big and tall; the ducks short and squat. They were hardly the scenario of Lorenz and his ducklings. It was only the threat of winter that drove the ducks from the pond, after which Waylon, finally, agreed to make the walk to the safety of the barn. There, he spent the entire winter in with the cows.

While no one in Vermont knows when spring will arrive, it always does. Sometimes the snow melts in late February, and we have bare ground and mud until May. Sometimes the grass grows right through the melting snow in May. Somehow the ducks knew when the ice started clearing from the ponds and, with perfect timing, they arrived to resume their rhythm of courting, nesting, and raising the next generation.

With spring, Waylon was freed from the barn and walked directly back to the pond, and his submerged rock, where he clearly meant to stay until winter chased him back. The ducks arrived shortly afterwards. There was no doubt that these were the same ducklings from the season before. They swam right out to Waylon, greeted him with quacks, wagged their feathered tails and took delight in finding their old friend. Waylon sang a happy song that night.

Of course, there was the courtship and the nesting and the next generation. Waylon was invited to take part in all of that. With several batches of tiny ducklings on the pond, the parents welcomed Waylon's watchful eye, as he busied himself as a baby sitter, educator and benevolent uncle. Konrad Lorenz would not have believed it!

Each year, for many years, this scenario was played out on my neighbor's pond. The ducks would arrive, surely several generations removed from the original group, and incorporate an old bachelor Chinese goose into the raising of their young. Waylon took his role seriously as the survival rate of ducklings on his pond surpassed that of others. The rock, large as it was, was sometimes pressed for space at night.

Each fall, when the light had faded and the cold winds started to blow, the ducks would say their farewell to Waylon and wing off to their other world. Waylon would honk for a day or two; his sad, lonely music telling us that winter was upon us. Then he would make his lonely walk back to the barn and the cows. He would wait there patiently, until spring, when his ducks would return.

PERSPECTIVE

"**H**ow are you doing, Dr. Parks," I asked, concerned that the wind and cold weather that jumped up during the day had taken a toll on him.

"Oh, I've been worse," he replied, "how about you?"

I was not about to indicate to an octogenarian that I was miserable, cold, hungry, stiff and my feet were numb when he looked so darn perky. None of us dared mutter a groan in the presence of such a man. We were getting a lesson in perspective.

When old horsemen find riding too testing for their bodies, they often turn to driving. I have no idea why since I have done both and find both challenging. But there it is, they drive.

Long-distance driving was invented just for this reason, to allow the old folk to continue to compete. Young folk joined in the sport also, but only to find their limitations far greater than those with whom they were competing. The old folk ran circles around us.

That day, the two front drivers had encountered a fallen tree across the trail. The only solution, other than turning around, was to move it. No way did they consider turning around. One held the horses, while the other heaved the tree off of the trail. We were dying to know who did which job. Did gallantry come into play or did they flip a coin?

'Why, I let Clara move the tree," explained Dr. Parks, "she's a lot younger than me."

She was seventy-six!

When you're young and you fall off a horse, you may break something. When you're my age and you fall off, you splatter.
~ Roy Rogers

Diary of a First Endurance Ride

Two Months Before the Ride:

Today I went to a clinic where a World Class endurance rider gave a talk about competing. She gave us all kinds of marvelous tips. The rules allow the rider to get off of the horse and walk or run alongside in order to give the horse a break. I have seen lots of pictures of this and think it would be pretty cool. I asked the World Class endurance rider how often she got off and ran. "Never," she said. "I feed the horse, clean up after the horse, train the horse; my horse had better carry me the whole way." I still think it will be cool to run with my horse and start training for my first ride.

One Month Before the Ride:

Yesterday I got myself a pair of stretch riding tights. I chose black, as I did not think I was ready for pink, turquoise or zebra stripes. That proved a singularly wise decision when I stuffed myself into them and caught sight of myself in the mirror. Yikes! I could not imagine what I would have looked like in zebra stripes! My hotshot endurance mentor is brave enough and skinny enough to ride in pink tights.

Three Weeks Before the Ride:

I spent the week getting a tee shirt that was the right length to disguise what the riding tights revealed. The husband, in not the most pleasant way, pointed out that I needed to pay attention to my underwear too.

The Week Before the Ride:

I am obsessed with what to take to the ride to care for my horse at the holds. I get advice daily from pink tights. She and the husband, my crew, were in agreement with the "less is better" concept. Easy for them to say, I would be the one to suffer, and I ignore them. The husband looks stressed over the growing pile in the barn.

The Day Before We Leave:
The electolyte thing is a real surprise for my horse. Open up, syringe in the salt. Yuck! He is not amused. I wonder if I will be able to catch him tomorrow? The trailer is packed and the truck is stuffed with camping gear.

Arriving at the Ride.:
The husband has taken charge of camping; thank goodness. Once a Boy Scout, always a Boy Scout. He is all excited about communing with nature and all that stuff. But, when we arrive at the ride-site, instead of seeing tents, we see huge live-in trailers with microwaves and television sets. We slink to an obscure camping site feeling very much the poor cousin.

The Evening Before the Ride:
The pre-ride briefing is just that, brief. We start at 5AM, have twelve hours to complete, there will be two holds, five fly-by locations and pulse criteria is sixty-four beats per minute. The husband is fervently writing all of this down not having a clue what it means. I am in shock as I realize that, at 5AM, it will still be dark! Did my Boy Scout bring a flashlight? There are lots of jokes about which rider will get lost; lost? I grab extra copies of the map. The meeting breaks up and everyone goes off to eat, drink, and be merry. They all act like this is one big party while I am so nervous I have been in the porta potty six times since we arrived.

The tent really is nice, and the husband conjures up a delicious Boy Scout dinner on his camp stove. Never mind those microwave dinners in front of a television; we are having a real endurance experience! My horse is somewhat amused with his accommodations. Pink tights is next to us and has my horse sharing a picket line with her horse. We did practice this at home, but I am sure my horse thought it one of those jokes humans play on horses. Tonight he realizes that this is no joke. He looks at the roomy portable paddocks that many other horses have in the same way we look at the live-in trailers.

Later That Night:
I can not sleep. I keep hearing my horse walking up and down his picket line and decide that neither one of us is going to sleep. Except for the husband who is snug as a bug in a rug in his Boy Scout sleeping bag. Until the first raindrop hits the tent. He bolts up like his pants are on fire

and scurries about "securing" camp - Boy Scout fashion. Thank goodness it is only a shower, but that is the end of any of us getting sleep.

Ride Day:

I crawl out of bed at 3:30AM. I have not been up at this hour since pulling an all nighter in college! My horse show days were looking so good, with classes scheduled for 9AM, a civilized time to be messing with a horse. But, I remind myself that this is a new horizon and scurry about feeding my horse and getting my tack together. I look over and pink tights is tacking up under the light of a flashlight held in her mouth. I look around and see that she has a lot of company doing that. I hope the husband does not suggest I do the same. Wisely, he does not and holds the flashlight for me.

We ride to the start where over fifty horses are milling around. Pink tights has promised to baby-sit me until the ride starts, but she has intentions of "running for it". I feel confident that I can handle this alone. After all, my horse has fox-hunted and is a very good boy about large groups of horses. Then the ride starts. My horse leaps forward in an attempt to keep up with pink tights' horse! We fly past the starting line, bucking through the mass of horses in fine style. The husband is aghast. I finally yank my horse to the side of the trail and hide until most of the riders pass. So much for all of those years of training!

I buddy up to the back of the ride where I find a lot of people grateful for a calmer pace. They are riders like me who simply want to get around, give their horses some experience and have fun. The sky lights up with dawn colors as we trot down the trail. Cool! The husband meets me on the trail at the first "flyby" and does his best to syringe some electrolytes into my horse. The horse is wise to this and the electrolytes miss his mouth and get me. Icky. The husband looks so flustered I don't dare ask for a clean shirt.

As we come into the first hold, the front running horses are just leaving. That, I learn, would be the last time I will see "the top ten." Pink tights is with them, waving madly at me as she flies by. The husband has my buckets and hay and grain all laid out in true Boy Scout fashion and is most helpful in holding the horse while I struggle with the stethoscope. By the time I get a heartbeat; the horse is about asleep. The vets are very nice to me, we get all "A's" on our vet card, and I am beaming. Before I know it, I am due to go out on the trail and late getting to the timer. I vow to do better at the next hold.

The trail gets a lot harder on the second loop. Hills, rocks and some tricky single track wooded trail that could take one's knees off. I decide, against the advice of the World Class endurance rider, to get off and walk a lot of it. I get a real sense of "endurance" by the end of that trail.

The next section of trail is not as hard, so I remount. It gets hot, so I decide to sponge water onto my horse. I use a cool trail sponge on a strap. I should have been able to dip it into the water, pull it up and sponge the horse from the saddle. Instead, my horse has a complete melt-down the moment I drop the sponge into the water. What dangling, horrible creature is attacking him? As my horse spins, I release the sponge, and it flies into the woods; never to be seen again. I manage to dismount in a rather unladylike manner and utter some rather unladylike words. I really liked that darn sponge.

The husband meets me two times on this trail and both times manages to squirt electrolytes everywhere but into the horse. Some of the other crew-members move farther away from us.

We get to a section of trail where the markers are not clear. My fellow riders enter into animated discussion as to which is the right way. "No problem," I say," I have a map!" I pull it out only to discover that, without my glasses, I cannot read it. Nor can anyone in our group. We sit and wait until someone "a bit younger" comes along to read it for us. How embarrassing.

The second hold seems a lot quieter than the first one. That is because, as the husband points out, most of the ride has already gone through. I am next to last. The husband points out that if I ride any slower I would soon be last. Ha, ha. I have been getting off to jog along with my horse all day in order to help him. What horsemanship! To my amazement, the husband comes up with a dose of electrolytes and pops it right into the horse's mouth. He explains that while I was dallying out on trail, he had plenty of time to ask questions and watch what other crews were doing for the horses. According to him, I had a lot to learn.

I set out on the last loop with the goal to pass someone, anyone, just so I can show the husband that I have it in me. We ride at a moderate pace and I spot two horses ahead on the trail. My horse, elated to have buddies again, catches up. The horses seem to enjoy each other's company so I decide to stay with them. My horse is moving forward smoothly, and I am enjoying the beautiful day spread out before me.

Suddenly I realize I am crossing the finish line, achieving the goal that I had been working so hard towards for months. I have tears streaming down my cheeks as I jog my horse for the vets for my completion. We did it! Fifty miles! And I am not last! We both look pretty good for the experience. Even the husband thinks so!

The Evening after the Ride:
I feel so good as I wrap my horse's legs and pack him into the trailer. The husband drives home and wakes me when we arrive. All efforts to get out of the truck on my own power fail me. My legs have decided to quit. The husband has to lift me out, and I hobble to the house and the couch where I remain all night.

Three Days After the Ride:
Today I managed to walk down the stairs without crying. I had been turning around and backing down them for two days. My horse has been trotting around the pasture with bouncing steps while I was crawling like a crab. The words of the World Class endurance rider came back to me; I can now see her point.

One Week After the Ride:
I can't believe what fun I had and I can't wait to do it again!

I've spent most of my life riding horses. The rest I've just wasted. ~
Anonymous

RAT

It never occurred to me that a rat was not everyone's idea of a pet; so cute and soft when they are little. I was ten when I named my first rat after a family friend. It had to be explained to her that it was meant as a compliment.

Terry The First was followed by Terry The Second and went on through Terry The Twenty. Rats followed me through my childhood, college and into my first career of teaching high school science. It is only recently that I have been "ratless", primarily due to the ferrets in my life. It is an understatement to say that the two are not compatible.

Rats are delightful pets. Mine lived in a cage next to my bed and would grasp the bars with their hand-like paws and push their inquisitive noses through, begging to come out to play. I built rat mazes and rat tunnels and spent countless hours playing with my rodent friends.

Rats do not live very long, but they live life to the fullest. Adorable, soft and full of fun, rattlings are hard to resist. However, their cuteness wears off pretty quickly as they come to resemble the pointy faced, stiff haired, shifty eyed image of the classic rat. It is a bum rap that rats were blamed for countless diseases, including bubonic plague, that not once, but twice, almost wiped out Europe. The truth is that rats died of the disease too. The true villain being the flea who carries the disease from one species to the other.

Rats have traveled with man through history, arriving in North America thanks to a free ride on a ship. They are so adaptive that practically every environment suits them. Their ability to survive every toxin man has ever thrown at them proves that eradication of the species will never occur. Man has not yet figured out that they will never beat the rat; they would be so much wiser to learn from them.

There are some famous rats: Ratatouille's rodent chef Remy, Harry Potter's Wormtail and the insatiable Templeton in Charlotte's Web. Like me, no doubt their creators played with pet rats as children.

I contracted chicken pox the day after my junior-prom, and was sent to bed with concern. Miserable, I sought the company of Terry The Fifth, and later must have dozed off. Our housekeeper, not a rat aficionada, was accompanied by our family doctor when she awakened me. Those were still the days of a doctor making house calls!

The concern over a chicken pox epidemic running through my high school class warranted the visit.

Taking his role seriously, he wanted to examine the extent of the pox and reached to pull down the covers. Terry The Fifth, having found a nice, warm snuggle spot next to my shoulder, popped up her head at the intrusion. From my perspective, lying in bed, I could only speculate why both faces gaped in frozen horror. It gave me just enough time to realize that Terry must be rescued before a non-rat-wise person stomped her.

No one, including my father, who learned of the incident through the exaggerated description from our housekeeper later that evening, thought it was funny. The incident was written up in a medical journal, which is why doctors no longer make house calls for fear of finding one's patient in a bed full of rats. An exaggeration, indeed.

THE UNSINKABLE FRAN GRANT

Iowe everything I know about conditioning and riding a distance horse to a remarkable lady named Fran Grant. A complete trail riding novice, I met her over a brisk phone call. She had only a few minutes to chat before leaving for a doctor's appointment to have her cast removed a week early so that she could ride that weekend. I must have commented that I thought her leg might be a bit weak for that, but she retorted, "No problem, I'll just wrap it with duct tape." And she did.

That Saturday, she rode 25 miles, served up dinner, gave out awards and started talking about the ride the next week. I dragged myself home and spent four days crawling up and down my stairs before my legs stopped cramping. It was at that point that I decided that if a woman twice my age with a broken leg could do this sport, so could I! Little did I know what I was in for.

A few weeks later I called her to take up her offer to ride together. She was only too happy to hear from me, but announced that unless I had a horseshoe driveway, she simply could not come. "Why?", I asked, somewhat bewildered.

"Because I can't back up a horse trailer."

What? Here was the winner of the Bruised Butt and Most Horse-shoes awards for three years running, which meant that she completed more rides than anyone else on the entire East coast, and she couldn't back her trailer. "They always have an area to turn around in," she shrugged in explanation. I later learned that she had not unhooked her trailer from the truck since the day she put them together, about eight years ago.

"Don't know how," was her matter of fact explanation.

By my offering to turn her trailer around for her, she agreed to a ride from my farm. I was excited to have the opportunity to pick up on any of the subtle little things that she did that made her a top contender in this sport. "Patton was one step from the can when I bought him," she told me with a sideways grin, "and he still is only one step from the can."

One look into this horse's eye told me that she was telling the truth.

The big-boned grey glared down at my quiet little Appaloosa, who was not at all sure this was such a nifty idea. He was massive in build, with an enormous head and huge feet, and did not seem to pay any attention to Fran at all. He dragged her out of the trailer; he dragged her to my barn; he dragged her out to the mounting block. This was, I reminded myself, the winner of countless one hundred mile rides.

Wow.

Mounting with a death grip on the reins, she whacked Patton with her crop and put her one spur into his side to start him off. "He only turns right, so I use the crop and spur to turn to the left," she explained as we took off down the trail. This was not quite what I had expected of such a well decorated pair, but I felt it best to nod in agreement with the wisdom of her riding techniques and off we went.

We had not gone more than a mile and were trotting along through the woods when I heard a thud behind me, followed by an expletive. I pulled up and turned, and there, lying flat on her behind, was my role model, with the reins still in a death grip and Patton attempting to drag her towards home. I made a mental note to re-check the ride results that put this woman at the top of almost every ride from Vermont to Florida. Maybe there was another Fran Grant? I smiled politely as I helped her get Patton back in order. We remounted and with a whack and a stab we continued our ride uneventfully.

For the next three years I spent a lot of miles riding with Fran. At competitions, she would ride behind me, using my Appaloosa as a brake so that she could give her arms a rest from reining in Patton. Patton never changed. I saw him step on her, drag her through the vet checks, drag her to and from the trailer, and otherwise try to do her in. Fran never changed. She would grab him by the bridle, swing right up and whack, stab him for twenty five, fifty or one hundred miles, whatever the case might be.

"You could ride this horse over a cliff and he would come up trotting," she'd say. I believed it. So did the judges. I watched Patton win his share of rides, while I was happy to be considered for a ribbon.

For that entire three-year period, Fran never stopped talking. She told me everything she knew and, when she was done, she started again. She knew a great deal. I tried to absorb what seemed important, but everything in distance riding is important, from what detergents to wash your saddle pad in, to how long before a ride one should shoe a horse. Fran taught me to pay attention to details. She knew Patton inside and out, up and down and sideways. She knew how many swallows of water he had taken, which leg he was favoring ever so slightly, and how many hairs had been rubbed by the girth.

She also knew how to care for riders. She shoved bananas into me as she expounded on the redeeming qualities of potassium. She recommended boots, britches and the right brand of underwear. When I made a mistake, she was right there to tell me about it. I smiled politely and absorbed it all.

One of my first rides was The Trail Trotters thirty-five mile ride that was notorious for its rocky, hilly terrain in French Creek State Park, PA. I knew I was in for a rough ride when the ride manager handed us all a slip of paper with two phone numbers. "The first is the number to call if your horse gets into trouble on the trail. It is the local vet clinic. The second is the number to call if you get lost or decide to quit. It is Dial-a-Prayer." I was not sure I was ready for this, but Fran would never hear of my backing out, so off we went.

I spent the first hour trying to pick my way across rock strewn trails, the second hour climbing and descending hills, the third hour trotting along an abandoned rail road bed, complete with ties, and the last hour slogging through mud. With eight miles yet to go, with only an hour left for us to finish, I was ready to quit.

Had I forgotten that the unsinkable Fran Grant was behind me? "Quit, don't be silly, just shut up and ride."

I had nowhere else to go anyway, so I put my game little mare behind the formidable Patton and we went like the devil for those last eight miles, made the time, vetted out in top form, and WON the ride. Fran was as surprised as I, but beginner's luck has to land on someone.

At seven o'clock the next morning I was still sleeping, dreaming that I was on a sandy beach with palm trees, a soft, offshore breeze, sipping a fruit cooler, when the phone rang.

"Hi, whatcha doing?" came the familiar voice.

Not about to be caught lagging around in bed while the day got away from me, I replied, "Just finishing the barn chores, why?"

"Oh, goody, let's go riding."

Riding? After thirty-five miles of torturous trail from the day before, she wanted me to go riding? Then I remembered that I had vowed not to let a woman twice my age get the best of me, "I'll be right over."

I was just dating the husband when Fran invited us to a party with her trail riding friends. Birds of a feather, the group was rather intimidating and had no qualms about checking the husband out to see if he was good enough for me. As we drove home, he quietly turned to me and asked, "Are all of your friends like that?"

Fran stopped riding the next year. She simply stopped. "I need to do something else," she said. That something else was playing bridge. I couldn't believe it. I had figured she would take up hang gliding, or water skiing, or polo, but playing bridge had never crossed my mind. Once again she knew what she was doing. She and Patton were going to bow out gracefully rather than try to push a few more miles. She still helped on rides and gave freely her advice to any that would listen. It was always gratifying to see her there, for I knew that all was in order, or else. Thirty years later, I'm still competing; I can still hear her every word when I ride down the trail. Thank you, Fran; I should also have had you teach me how to play bridge.

Taking It Slow

"**M**oving cattle," instructed Jeff, "is a lot like getting ninety psychotic people, each wrapped in a bubble, to go where you want them. Push to close to that bubble, and you will quickly find out what I mean."

We were sitting on our horses in the middle of Montana, having offered to help move a herd five miles to a new range. It was a new adventure for the husband and me, but being long time horse people, we were aware that not everything might go smoothly. Jeff made that very clear.

Nothing could compare to being on a good horse on the open range with snow topped mountains looming in the background. We were viewing land that had been cow country for hundreds of years, and performing a task that had not changed much in hundreds of years. For just that short time, we were going to taste the life of a cowboy.

Our cowboy was Jeff. He did not have to try to be a cowboy; he just was. He could not help but look good on a horse and his skills were impressive. He loved his life and his job, and it showed. What a treat to see him in action.

As the cows moved off with their calves, forty-six pair, the size of the herd took form. The horses took the work seriously, keeping their eye on the cattle, moving and stopping at the slightest cue. They knew how to push, back off, push again. It was slow, but engaging work. I was soon to learn a new declaration; as slow as moving a herd of cows with calves five miles up hill.

Slow is crucial. Rush a cow and she will pay you back by bolting for the first place that looks better than where you are standing. Sometimes that could be right back to where the herd started, certainly not a progressive step. At certain intervals we closed gates behind us; insurance.

As the day wore on, it was entertaining to observe Jeff. He used an endless reservoir of vocabulary to get the cows to move.

"Come on, mama."

"Let's get up there."
"Bring that baby along."
"Git to your mama."
"Git up."
"Git."
"Shush."
"Tch, tch."

Eventually Jeff resorted to just sounds.
Sounds such as tics, whistles, clucks, hisses, grunts, sighs. It was endless. I could not even begin to emulate him and did not attempt to try. He got off his horse and walked. He got back on and rode. He unfurled his rope and recoiled it. He took off his hat, put it back on. He slapped his leg, his horse, his saddle. Occasionally he would wave his arm about. It was fascinating to watch.

When the cows finally reached their destination high on the dry range, we all relaxed and complimented each other on a job well done. I could not help but comment on Jeff's performance and ask him what action in particular moves the cows best.

"None of them," he commented slyly, "I do it to keep from getting bored."

So much for cowboy technique.

Always drink upstream from the herd.

No Goat

One is either a goat person, or not. Goats sense this. There is a little test everyone gets to do with goats, one that either proves one to be adept at contact sports, or not.

Gotee was perhaps the most calculating goat in my life. His sense of timing and humor caused him to have all sorts of adventures. There was the time a carpenter, declaring himself a goat person, worked all day without incident; until he climbed up a ladder. Thinking he was pushing his luck, I expressed concern, but he assured me that he and Goatee had worked things out. That was until he stepped down from the ladder. Goatee reached over and pulled out the bow that held up his workbelt. It dropped with a thud, spewing tools everywhere, much to the anguish of the carpenter.

The husband had a cousin. She was raising a grandson who might have been called autistic. He was charming, but Foster only expressed himself with single words, if that. He loved coming to the farm to pet the soft noses of the horses and play with the kittens. We would hear his laughter and know that he was having the time of his life when a horse picked a treat gently from his hand. Or when a kitten would ride on his shoulder, purring in contentment. It was a good place for him, one that offered unconditional acceptance of his odd ways, something he did not always enjoy with his peers.

When it comes to little people, defined as anyone eye level or less, goats have a real need to knock them over. Not really butting, but bumping, just enough to see the child roll to the ground. The tough ones get up, only to be bumped to the ground again. And again. The tough ones do not quit very easily, much to the delight of the goat. Parents usually end the game, berating the goat, and the child, for thinking this acceptable behavior. The ones that cry get snatched up, the goat gets penned up, and better care was taken on the whereabouts of the goat at the next visit.

We were somewhat apprehensive about Foster and the goat, being that they were about equals in size, but Foster remained determined to pet him. Goatee, somewhat taken back by such a fearless approach of a little person, played along. Lulled into thinking that everything was satisfactory we wandered off a bit.

The first time Foster hit the ground I am sure he thought it was funny, and being tough, he bounced right up. The second time he hit the ground it was not as funny. Nor was the third. At this point, Goatee was having such an enjoyable time playing with Foster that he would bump him before he even attempted to get up. Resourceful, Foster started rolling on the ground to get away; that brought the game to a new level. That is about the time we turned our attention in their direction.

Foster was pretty dirty but not overly upset about the experience. He gave a few nods about where he had a little cut, but he proved to be a pretty resilient four-year-old boy. My concern was that he might have lost his connection with the farm animals, so I offered him a kitten. He broke into a big grin as I placed the kitten on his lap and he sat thoughtfully, petting her, for a minute or so. Then he stood, walked over to where Goatee had been imprisoned in a horse stall, and gave the goat his full attention.

Foster had always struggled with words that never came out right. He felt, perhaps for the first time, an urgency to communicate clearly to us. Not until this day did he feel the want to express a need to survive. That need, announced with perfect diction, was, "NO GOAT!"

His first sentence! And certainly not his last. Foster was on his way into the world, thanks to that goat.

DASH TO DAHSHUR

I was trying to absorb every detail of the moment as I trotted past the Great Pyramids on my way into the Sahara Desert. I was mounted on a chestnut Arabian, the husband on a lovely grey. A friend who lived just outside of Giza was guiding us and two other guests. We were in Egypt!

We had spent the first week in tourist boats floating down the Nile and stopping to see the wonders of Aswan, Luxor and the Valley of the Kings. To our delight, we were transported to many of the sites via horse and carriage. Horses and donkeys move Egypt. We even got to see a donkey barber shop were the animals are taken to be clipped. Various symbols and designs are integrated into the coat to help with the donkey's performance. The more symbols; the more difficult the donkey.

Our second week was spent at the home of our very gracious friend who offered guided horse tours. We met her through the sport of endurance riding so we had quite a bit in common. She had a wonderful stable of Arabian horses and had asured us twenty miles of desert riding and our day was just unfolding. It held the promise of being a most spectacular day on horseback.

It was necessary to thread ourselves through the alleys of native Egyptian houses in order to reach the desert. Irrigation canals from the Nile served as the water source for gardens and fields and were bordered by towering eucalyptus trees. The crowding of people and plants and animals to the water was in contrast to the vast open desert. Where the water stopped, the desert began.

The desert was imposing. Three thousand miles of sand lay before us. There was remarkably little out there but sand. Rising above the desert were the wondrous pyramids of Giza, the Pyramid of Khafre and the Pyramid of Khufu, and The Sphinx. We had ridden camels around that area the day before and touched the ageless stones, feeling the centuries in our fingertips. Now we were about to see what most tourists do not. We were riding to Dahshur and would pass by the Red Pyramid, the Bent Pyramid, the Step Pyramid and the Black Pyramid. We would most likely be the only ones there, other than the occasional student involved in an archeological dig, as these pyramids enjoyed anonymity from the tourist crowds.

As we trotted past the congested parking lots and queued up tourists, we swung our mounts south to the silhouette of the Red Pyramid, our first destination. Our guide, knowing that we were experienced riders, suggested we allow the horses a little canter to stretch their legs. What a grand idea, we thought, as did the other two riders. One was an experienced event rider and the other a life long rider. What better way to start our ride?

We were off! Within ten seconds, it was apparent to us that our guide's concept of "a little canter" was more like the start of the Kentucky Derby. Within those ten seconds I reviewed my options; go with it and hope for the best or attempt to control an animal who I did not know and on which I had spent but fifteen minutes. I went with it. The husband, however, opted for the later choice, so I blew by him like a bullet. The other two riders were struggling to stay back with him.

With three thousand miles of sand before us, there was plenty of room to run out the horses. However, the Sahara desert is not a beach; it is the result of thousands of years of erosion of rocks. The "sand" is very, very old sand, more like fine talc. Mixed in with that are millions of rocks on their way to becoming sand. From my pseudo jockey position over my horse's neck, the rocks were in clear view, some of which my steed was swerving to avoid, some of which he soared over in a low, broad-jump fashion. It was apparent that this was not his first "little canter" in the desert.

As I looked down at the desert sliding by me, I caught glimpses of items one does not normally see. A short distance from the Great Pyramids we started across a thatch work of carefully laid out heaps of sand with alleys in between. The piles were not just sand and rock; they contained shards of pottery and more than a few bones. Now and again I would catch sight of a skull. A human skull. This was the dumping ground for archeological digs from the tombs and pyramids! I absolutely had no wish to come off of my horse in such a place.

Our guide's horse, happy as the wind, was not giving up much of his lead. I could see the little poufs of beige dust

37

coming from his flying feet as he led us further and further from the Pyramid of Khafre. I was thinking that perhaps, at this speed, I would see the next four pyramids in record time, if I got to see them at all.

Fast as my horse was traveling; he was no match racer. Coming from behind were the other two riders, horses stretched out at a full run, ears pinned and not giving an inch to the other. As happy as they were, their riders were terrified. Having called upon all of their skills, they had come to realize that nothing was going to stop this race. They were now riding in survival mode, the girl hugging against the horse's neck, reins thrown loose; I could not even see her face as she flew by me.

The young man was exactly the opposite. He had his feet jammed forward in the stirrups and was leaning back on the reins with everything he had. It was doing no good, but he seemed loath to abandon that position for anything else. He looked as much like a human clothespin on a horse as anyone could. I think perhaps he was screaming too, but the running horses made too much noise for me to hear anything over the pounding hooves and laboring lungs. They were bound to catch our guide at the rate they were running. I had to wonder if the horses might pass her and run all they way to Morocco.

The husband's horse pulled alongside me and seemed happy to match the pace of mine, who, at a full out gallop, seemed slow compared to the others. In comparison, it did actually feel like a "little canter." It took about two miles for the horses in front of us to run themselves out, coming down to a nice canter and then an easy trot. By the time we caught up with them everyone seemed fine, although the young man was a bit twitchy. Our guide, satisfied that the horses had been given their promised exercise, settled down to a nice trot as we turned south towards the looming Red Pyramid with the Bent Pyramid and Step Pyramid in view. They were so spectacular that it was easy to forget the thrilling start.

I found one way to fly; on the back of a horse !!!

No Pets Allowed

"Come stay with us, I could really use your help," begged my getting-more-pregnant-by-the-minute friend, Liz. "I'm still fine with the indoor chores, but this belly is getting to be a bother doing the outside ones." An invitation to spend a cold winter in upstate New York would not have been so inviting were it not for the special nature of Liz's household. I packed up my worldly possessions, two horses and a cat, and was there by the weekend.

Liz had swerved off the road to becoming a New York debutante for the world of animals. As her mother politely put it, "She moved from a penthouse to a zoo." Exotically beautiful with an engaging smile, instead of continuing classes at NYU, she talked her way backstage at the Metropolitan Opera House during "La Traviata" and went home with the horse. The horse lived in New Jersey.

The horse did not live alone. Pfeiffer's Animal Farm was home to a menagerie of working and retired theatrical animals. The most famous was Leo the MGM lion, who roared at the start of every MGM movie. Leo had lived wild in Africa before becoming a movie star, the story of which was told with increasing embellishment by his handler, Volney Pfeiffer, every time he was asked over the next forty years. I did see photographs of that famous safari and have no doubt that it was quite the adventure. Leo was old and toothless by the time I met him, but he still had the same effect when he roared.

I met Liz while trying to get my horse past the lion cage on route to my friend Linda's house. Suburbia did not offer a lot of choices as to where I could ride and one of the few trails I used came out through the large animal enclosures at Pfeiffer's. I had a choice of passing a buffalo, a herd of reindeer, a polar bear, or the old lion. The horse preferred the lion as he was asleep most of the time.

With our mutual love of animals, Liz and I became devoted friends.

By the time I moved in with her in upstate New York, Liz's animal fetish had reached an all time high: her ten year old daughter had a young wild boar that she rode through the house, her six year old daughter had a chimpanzee, the "house cat" was a declawed and quite tame bob cat, a red rat snake wintered in the hall closet, there was a great horned owl in the laundry room, and Liz was raising a baby elephant in the basement. Outside there was a herd of reindeer, a herd of horses, the parents of the wild boar in the house, a llama, a Kodiak bear and an emu. What a marvelous place!

Understandably, Liz's mother did not visit too often. Even when Liz named the elephant Mignon, after her, she just shook her head, convinced that her baby girl had been switched at birth with one from a gypsy caravan. Mignon was Liz's pride and joy. Baby elephants are cute as can be and extremely social. Mignon followed Liz everywhere, shuffling along, stuffing her trunk into nooks and crannies and snorting out her opinion of what she found there. She climbed into the mini van and rode to the airport to pick up Liz's husband when he traveled, and was a familiar sight at baggage claim, swinging her trunk and rocking her head at the sights and sounds no other elephant had ever come upon.

Most certainly, Liz did encounter a little resistance in bringing an elephant through the doors of the Newark International Airport. It was pointed out to her that there was a "No Dogs" sign clearly visible at the entrance. "I saw that," she retorted, "obviously Mignon is not a dog." The new sign said NO PETS. To that Liz countered with, "Not a pet, she is an elephant." They were happy when Liz moved to upstate New York.

Mignon had outgrown the house and was situated in a large pen in the basement. She spent days outside, but on the cold winter nights she was brought into the house. The path to the basement was through the kitchen which caused some memorable forays should she manage to open wide the faucets in the sink as she passed by. One could not stop to turn off the water without losing the elephant and by the time she slid down the stone steps into the basement to her pen, the water pressure on the entire farm dropped to next to nothing. It was unfortunate timing to be taking a shower when the elephant was moved.

The water was pulled from the well with an old pump located in an old barn. It was a lovely long-standing three story barn, the lower level built into the bank, the second level even with the road and the third level high above for hay storage. My horses lived in the lower level, with access to a stone walled courtyard that offered protection from the wind and a southern exposure. I suppose that is why the emu liked it too.

I discovered the emu in the lower barn after tossing some hay into the rack against the back stonewall and flushing out a six foot, eighty pound bird. He was pretty upset with me, demonstrated by the gyrations of his neck and legs, as he leapt into the air flapping his vestigial wings and hissing bird obscenities. I apologized for I truly had not seen him. Amazing as that might sound, to miss a six foot, eighty pound bird, as emus collapse themselves into a rather obscure brownish ball of feathers by tucking up their legs and wrapping that long, snaky neck into the ball of feathers.

For the rest of the winter, the emu took residence in the hayrack. My horses accepted this as normal for whatever reason I never could fathom. The sight of a wild turkey while riding through the woods would produce a leap of fright, yet an emu, sleeping inches from their muzzles as they munched on hay, was fine. They actually became friends.

I discovered the extent of this friendship when I saddled up my mare for a ride on a particularly striking winter day. I put a lead line on the second horse in order to bring him along for some much needed exercise, and looked forward to exploring the farther reaches of the five hundred acre farm. I was just out of view of the barn when my mare flicked back an ear and I heard a peculiar noise coming from behind me. I glanced back; saw nothing. A short while later the same thing happened. As I turned onto a wooded trail, I glimpsed a six-foot, eighty-pound form running easily along through the trees, giving a little flap here and there as if those wings could help it along. The emu was with us! Winter did not offer up too many riding opportunities, but I never went without the company of the bird.

As Liz's increasing belly assigned more and more chores to me, I was busy from dawn to dusk. I would get the girls off to school and then start the morning chores of moving the elephant out to her run, throwing the owl a piece of chicken neck, a second one to the bob cat and checking on the semi-hibernation state of the snake. Periodically he would wake up and slither around looking for a handout, which could be alarming for repairmen or meter readers. We liked to keep tabs on him

The elephant took up a considerable part of my day. First, imagine cleaning up after an elephant! Still a baby, along with her ration of oranges, bananas, apples, and monkey chow – all of which she individually stomped into a flat pancake before eating - was a bottle. Mignon loved that bottle and would wrap her trunk around your head and neck and sway as she drank. It was impossible not to sway with her. Deep down she would make a sound like a kitten purring, a semblance of the ear splitting roar that she was capable of when upset.

Her voice at that age resembled more of a lion than an elephant.

One of the requirements after evening feeding was to allow Mignon to suck my thumb while she rocked and swayed and took me with her until she felt sleepy. Sometimes that could take an hour. The only other animal that could hold a thumb like that was a lion cub. Once they had it, you had to wait until they dozed off to get it back. Sometimes Liz would come down and sit while Mignon ran her trunk over Liz's face, blowing elephant kisses and purring. I was only beneficial to Mignon for food, clearly Liz was her mother figure. Often I would hear Liz call goodnight to Mignon from upstairs and hear the elephant gently roar back.

My chores would then move outside to hay the reindeer, horses and llama and throw kitchen scraps to the boars. The bear was out of bounds, not because she was difficult, but because it was imperative for Liz's husband to feed and handle her to keep their relationship on good terms. He was filming Hamm's beer commercials, which required him to drive a jeep, paddle a canoe, and hike through the woods in complete control of that bear. They were truly impressive together, but I did not miss that it was a particularly significant relationship that needed no interference from me.

Last on my list of chores was the chimpanzee who had a cozy little room in the pump house part of the big barn. I arrived with sliced apples, monkey chow, a peanut butter sandwich, raisins, a cup of hot coffee, cream and sugar, and of course, several bananas. The youngest daughter had carefully instructed me as to the order in which her chimpanzee preferred to eat. First was the cup of coffee. She then disassembled the peanut butter sandwich, licked off the grape jelly, put the sandwich back together, and ate it. The money chow was unceremoniously pushed to the side while she picked at raisins and apples. Taking another sip of coffee, she started on the bananas, peeling them carefully before eating each one. When she was done, she ate the peels.

Settling back from her meal, she would gesture to me and offer a piece of monkey chow. Obviously I did not rank high enough, in her opinion, to rate the yummy stuff, although the youngest daughter did tell me that once she was offered a raisin, a high compliment. Not wanting to offend, I accepted and discovered just why monkey chow was not high on her list of dining fare.

If I sat long enough with her, she would sidle up to me and check my face. Carefully, she examined every freckle, gently flicking a finger at anything that did not seem to belong there. Slowly, she rolled up my knitted woolen hat, moving from my face to my hairline to my ears and to the back of my neck. With her face inches from mine, she groomed me as if I were a fellow chimp; finally satisfied, she would jam my hat back on my head, finish her coffee, and hand me back the cup. Now you understand why an opportunity to spend a winter in upstate New York in the company of Liz's animals was something I would not have turned down.

Spring was feeling close, and Liz was waiting daily for the arrival of her third child. I was busier than ever, so perhaps I didn't notice the absence of the six foot, eighty-pound bird until that evening. Liz's husband was not due home until late which left the girls and me to search that colossal old barn. Even with the aid of flashlights, we knew it would be extremely difficult to spot a ball of feathers. We came up empty.

It was not as if he could fly away; he had to have walked. One would think that someone would have noticed a six-foot, eighty-pound bird walking down the road. But they had not. The neighbors, the closest being half a mile away, were alerted should they encounter such a bird while doing morning chores and have a heart attack. Not everyone was as used to Liz's menagerie as we were.

By late afternoon the next day the bird was still missing, and we were genuinely worried. The emu was used to the soft life, knowing little of the dangers of running wild in a country full of coyotes and bear. It was Liz who finally came up with the plan. "Perhaps your horses could find him," she suggested, "they were such buddies." So, into the saddle I went and, with five hundred acres of farmland to cover in the short time before dark, I did not dally.

As I rode through the soft footing of the thawing hay fields, I kept an eye on my mare's ears, watchful for the familiar flick when she knew the emu was following us. There it was. Nothing in sight, but I thought I heard a sound. Another flick. And another. Then, from the underbrush, popped my six foot, eighty pound bird who failed to produce the effect a ten pound wild turkey would have from my horse, again to my wonderment. The emu was incredibly happy to see my mare, hopping about in emu gyrations and clacking his beak in emu greeting. My mare nickered back.

I felt left out of this happy reunion, but I too was happy. Then it occurred to me that I was every bit of two miles from the barn, and had to get my feathered friend back before dark. Still running in emu circles and clacking, he was entirely wrapped up in the excitement of seeing my mare. As he ran by, for the umpteenth time, I recalled a snippet of emu knowledge that Liz had shared with me as I had left the house. "Emus are birds, take away their sight and they sit quietly," she had instructed. I had not totally understood the value of her advice until now. I pulled off my woolen hat, aimed carefully, and dropped it over the head of the passing emu. He stopped on the spot.

My mare and I were both relived to have put the gyrations to an end. Thinking that five minutes were enough to calm the bird, I pulled off the cap. Into the air he leapt and continued, as if there had been no interval, his wild dance of happiness. Evening was not waiting for me, so I dropped the cap back over his head, and again, he stopped on the spot.

Sightless, the emu could not follow me back to the barn yet, given his sight, he could not stop expressing his joy over seeing us. I slid down from my mare and ran one rein around the long, snaky neck of the bird. I stepped forward; both the mare and emu came along. We had a rickety start, my having to keep steady pressure on the rein around the bird's neck for him to understand which direction to turn and the mare having to keep her reserve every time the bird bumped into her flank. We slowly progressed and, before darkness completely swallowed us, came into the light of the barn and the welcome shed with the hayrack.

When I finally pulled off the cap, the emu was utterly relaxed and blinked at me as if I had just appeared. He was hungry, tired, and perhaps remorseful for putting us all though this, but it did not show. Into the hayrack he jumped, folding up his legs and wrapping up his neck until he was an almost indiscernible ball of brown feathers, as if nothing had happened. Thankfully, he never went missing again.

Spring came, the baby came, and I returned to New Jersey; but not without the memories of the most out of the ordinary winter ever.

PANTY HOSE

I had a friend named Jerry who competed his stallion, "Irene," in fifty-mile endurance races. Jerry was an accomplished rider and a lot of fun, nevertheless not too many of us ever got to ride with him because Irene was not very sociable. When on a ride in Florida, Irene returned camp without Jerry. We rushed out to find him. There was Jerry, where Irene had planted him, lying in the sand with a fractured leg. His first concern was the horse, who, we assured him, was fine. His second concern was whether or not we felt we could get his jeans off before we took him to the hospital. Strange request until he explained that he rode with panty hose under his jeans and that he had no wish to explain that in the emergency room. We, especially the men folk, sympathized with this plight, but could do nothing to help him. "Well," he said, "perhaps they won't notice." We doubted it.

When the weather report for an upcoming one hundred mile ride offered nothing but rain, cold rain and possible snow flurries, I thought about Jerry. Jerry knew what he was doing; wearing panty hose added a thin, slippery layer under riding tights that not only helped keep one warm, but eliminated chaffing by wearing wet clothing. I got to thinking that perhaps panty hose would be a smart idea and I shared the thought with the husband.

"Really," he said, showing his complete ignorance of panty hose.

"Yep, remember Jerry, he always wore them when he rode."

"The guy that went to the hospital?"

"The same."

"I wonder how that went for him," mused the husband who was visualizing Jerry's nurses' surprise to find a big, strapping man in panty hose in their emergency room. He was sure there were comments.

I, of course, did not own a pair of panty hose. I had managed to work out a wardrobe that eliminated the need even for formal occasions. I had suffered in panty hose plenty from fourth to eighth grade. The sixties defiant wardrobe was welcomed primarily on the basis that it did not include panty hose.

The husband lived for the weather report. He often would announce the day's anticipated weather and stick his head out at ten o'clock to verify that it, indeed, had started to rain at the time predicted. The weatherman had skunked me so many times that I was

45

an acerbic skeptic in contrast to the husband's faithful following.

Two weeks before our next one-hundred mile ride, the husband had scoured the weather predictions like a scholar. A twenty per cent chance of rain had built to a fifty percent chance of rain and eventually promised a day of downpour. By evening it was not only going to rain, there was a possibility of snow. I just shrugged, having been an endurance rider long enough just to accept what came. However, the husband was also riding this ride and he was not fond of getting wet.

"So," the husband asked rather coyly, "just where does one get panty hose?"

I shot him a quick look, realizing that he was not asking for my needs, but for his! I just lost it, right then and there, and called my girlfriends to tell them. I am sure they called more girlfriends. I was not much help.

"Fine," said the husband, "have your fun. I will get them myself."

This only led to more phone calls.

To the husband's credit, he did march into a store with full intent of purchasing panty hose. He brought along a guy friend for help, although I am not sure why he thought it would be helpful. Perhaps more for moral support? I would have given anything to be there; it probably went like this.

"Wow, look at how many different kinds there are!"

"Yeah, I think I want the reinforced toe, whatever that means. I sure don't want my foot busting through half way through the ride."

"Good thinking. About the sizes, what do you think?"

"Cripes, they have petite, medium and Queen size. What do you think they mean by "Queen?"

"I dare you to ask!"

"What ever happened to 'large'?

"Ever call a woman 'large'?

"Oh brother, I can't believe I am buying Queen size panty hose!"

But he did. And he bought a pair for me too.

The weatherman was spot on with the forecast. We both wiggled into our panty hose feeling decidedly smug that we had thought ahead. We would not suffer like those who had not had such foresight. We were so darned smart.

The husband prayed the entire fifty miles that he would not suffer the fate of Jerry and have to explain his attire to some nurse somewhere. The panty hose did their job and he finished his ride congratulating himself, although certainly not sharing his secret with the world.

I too was thinking just how clever I was. The panty hose were keeping me warm and my legs were escaping the nasty little rubs often incurred in conditions such as this. What I did not expect, after sixty miles, was for it to stop raining. What? Where was that weatherman? Welcome weather as it was, it revealed a flaw in my brilliant plan.

Riding one hundred miles has nothing to do with just sitting on a horse. The rider is constantly moving with the various rhythms of his mount, up and down, up and down. Movement causes friction; friction causes heat. I was becoming more and more aware of a burning sensation in my thighs. Not the part that was in contact with the saddle, but rather the upper part of my thigh. That was weird. The more I rode on, the worse it got bringing me to the point of wanting to do something about it. Still, I could not put my finger on the cause; just what was it? Why did I have the feeling that I had experienced such a discomfort before? Think, think, what was it?

In sixth grade, panty hose was the rage that replaced knee socks for any girl who wanted to look up to date. It gave us bare legs with a false tan and smooth texture that was, for sure, "in." The panty hose went on in the morning, regardless of weather; hot, cold, wet, it did not matter. It was the hot, humid weather that brought out the evil of panty hose; friction burn. Synthetic against skin, add exercise and hot weather, and one's thighs would burn as if on fire. Ahh, now I knew what was wrong with me, the panty hose had started to dry, and tighten, on my legs!

Fifteen miles later I arrived at the mandatory hold with only one thought on my mind; get out of the panty hose! I entrusted my horse to the husband and went straight to a friend's camper to strip down. Rain coat first. Now for the half chaps. Boots. Boots took a while; the laces were still wet as were the boots. Socks peeled back and dragged off of my feet with enormous effort. Wet socks just do not come off easily. Now, off with my riding tights, ugh, they were stuck to the panty hose and half way down just stopped. Help! I needed help! I stuck my head out of the camper and yelled for anyone with a free hand. One of the guys jumped in. Whatever, he was help.

"Grab this," I instructed, realizing that the carnage of my discarded attire must have appeared a bit alarming to my rescuer.

"Just a second here," he said, "what are we doing?"

"The goal," I panted, "is to get me out of these pants!"

"Uh huh," he nodded. "The last time I helped a girl out of her pants was..."

"Just pull!" I interjected, and with that was free of my tights.

Finally down to the panty hose, both my helper and I were amazed at the tenacity with which they held onto my legs. Like a python about to lose his dinner, they fought back. "Get a knife, get a gun, I

47

don't care which," I gasped, "but get them off!"

I lay on the floor with my thighs glowing red from the nylon burn, facing the task of redressing in four minutes, or less, as the hold time was running out. I slathered my legs like a greased pig, yanked on my tights, jammed on my boots and half chaps, and got back on my horse.

"Ah," I said, as the horse moved out under me, "that feels a lot better!"

I could have avoided such a mishap had I only paid more attention in sixth grade, but then again, that was some time ago.

TRAPPED IN A TRUCK

If one were unlucky enough to sit on our sofa when the dachshund was "in residence," one would quickly understand why dachshunds were dropped into badger holes. The badger did not stand a chance; neither did anyone sitting on that sofa.

Prairie was an impulse acquisition in Wisconsin. Her full name was Prairie du Chien, Wisconsin, after the town from which she hailed. She was six weeks old and looked more like a gerbil than a puppy. Outrageously cute, she even managed to charm the ticket counter lady at the airport. Our timing in flying a dog was the same week that Zsa Zsa Gabor's Yorkies had escaped their carry-on bag and terrorized the First Class passengers on her flight. Dogs on flights were in lock down.

The airline's solution to those wanting to fly dogs in the cabin with passengers was to design a mandatory carrier that no dog could fit into. "Sure we fly dogs," they said, "as long as they can fit into this!" It would have been just as easy to squeeze an elephant into one's purse. The lady at the ticket counter diabolically showed us the carrier with full expectation that the dog in question would be sequestered securely in the hold of the plane. But when I reached into my pocket, revealed a ten ounce "gerbil," and demonstrated that not only could she fit into the carrier, she could gallop around in it, she was stymied.

Prairie should have had one of those magnetic maps of America on which one placed a state every time one visited. She would have had two provences in Canada too. Prairie went into a form of hibernation when on the road. Snuggled into any item available, a jacket, sweatshirt or blanket, she would sleep "the sleep of a thousand years."

Dragging her out at gas stations for a "walk and pee" was not her idea of fun. She would reluctantly walk across the pavement to the landscaped bushes and trees that gas stations are known to have. There she would stand and look out at the horizon as if expecting something to appear.

"Come on, Prairie," the husband would coo. He loved that dog. "You must be ready to explode, surely you have to pee?"

Continued staring.

"Please?"

Nothing.

"Pretty please?"

In the time required for that dog to pee I would have filled the truck with fuel, washed the windshield, fed the horses in the trailer, gone into the station to pee myself, and come back to no husband, no dog, at the truck. I probably could have had the tires rotated on both the truck and the horse trailer in the time it took Prairie to ultimately visit nature. She would come trotting back to the truck, all proud of herself, and we would finally get back on the road. Given that, could that dog make it through the night?

The only thing that got Prairie's attention when we traveled was food. Bring food into the truck and she bolted out of her trance with exuberant passion. It was not a sound idea to place the food anywhere but on the dashboard and, even then, there were several occasions when the food had to be rescued. We learned to eat pretty fast.

We were in Bethune, South Carolina, for a one-hundred mile ride. Bethune is a pretty funky Southern town where one of the best breakfast's you can imagine is served out of the local gas station. It was Thanksgiving weekend, and we were crewing for our friend, Steve. We had driven the horses down with Prairie. She had slept for two days and was not exactly thrilled with spending another day in a truck driving around to meet Steve at various check-points on the trail. I could see her point.

Crewing on a one-hundred mile ride entails a lot of grunt work to move hay, water, grain, blankets, buckets, chairs, ice chests and perhaps a tent. Steve, although he considered himself a minimalist, had a commanding amount of "stuff" following him. Steve's wife, Dinah, and the husband and I had been at the task since six that morning while the dachshund slept in the truck. Other than an occasional walk, she had little interest in her people at work. We were no fun at all; even less fun when it started to rain.

It was dark by the time we had reorganized all of our equipment under the tent. The rain was steady but not as unpleasant as we had anticipated. It was about that time that we noticed that the truck was missing.

Having had enough crew food for a day, Steve's wife had decided to head for the local gas station to get some real food and bring it back for all of us. She grabbed her dog, an especially polite Pomeranian, and took off in the truck. About half way to Bethune, she discovered that she was not alone.

Her first hint was that the Pomeranian was as far away from her as possible, huddling against the passenger door. No coaxing could bring him near. Perplexed, she patted the blanket next to her for him to come, and heard a low, threatening growl. She almost drove off of the road. The growling continued until a small, pointy, head popped out and put the stare on Dinah. "Yikes," she said.

Dinah knew only too well what it was like to share a sofa with Prairie and here she was, trapped in a truck with the dachshund next to her. Having discovered a rattlesnake under that blanket would have been less unnerving. "Yikes!"

The Pomeranian was whimpering. Dinah kept driving. Having been so rudely disturbed, Prairie nosed herself out of the blanket and crawled into Dinah's lab. "YIKES!" Frozen in fear, Dinah kept the truck on the road but only with sheer determination and grit. Still disturbed about being aroused from her nap and wondering just where the heck she was going, Prairie climbed up onto the door armrest and peered out of the window.

"It was like she was driving," told Dinah later, "like she had taken over the controls and I was at her command."

Any attempt to move the dachshund was met with a deep-seated growl. Dinah was no fool; she had heard that growl on the couch before! She found the first place to turn around, drove straight back to the check-point, rolled down the window and yelled to us for help.

The husband, he loved that dog, ran to Prairie's, not Dinah's, rescue.

"Oh, oh," he muttered, cuddling the little pooch, "we were so worried when we discovered you were gone. Poor, poor, little Prairie."

Dinah never again got into a truck without first checking for the presence of our pooch. And, she never, ever sat on our couch again.

Even the tiniest dog is still a wolf at heart.

SOARING WITH EAGLES

The man, a Native American, knelt on the ground, head bowed, with his thumb and two fingers balancing him against the grey dirt. He did not move, his entire concentration on the spot of ground where he knelt. Behind him, in the pen constructed just for this purpose, stood a piebald stallion whose concentration was exactly the opposite. His head up, he stared out onto the Montana hills, down through the river valley, and beyond, to open land where a horse could run forever. The only movement was the slight rise of a wisp of hair from the horse's mane in the wind. Everyone waited, quietly.

The group of us was a unique collection of equine professionals gathered from around the world for a weekend conference of interaction and exchange of ideas. There were some pretty high power folk there, some jostling for their position in the conference, some actually squaring off with their "competition" over who had the best technique. There was so much diversity in the group that not one theory of horse training could possibly come to the front. Yet many were so accustomed to having a following, of being a leader, that they felt uncomfortable at times in the group.

There was no clear leader here, other than our hostess, who threw this mix of talented and opinionated people together. She was standing back to see what became of us, with the hope that we would carry away something meaningful. The husband and I decided that hers was the best approach, and sat back to observe.

The man raised his head, the action revealing his face to us, and smiled, "Now he is ready." As he spoke these words, the horse left his fantasy of freedom and walked quietly to the center of the pen and touched the man on his shoulder. The man stood up, stroked the horse, and started to talk.

It was his voice that caught me. He drew me in as he told the story of how The People tamed the horse, about the circle of life that surrounds man and the horse, and how crucial it is to see that when asking the horse to become tame, to become the instrument of man. The horse stood by him, moving his head from time to time as if to agree with what was being said. As the story drew on, I started to notice the scars on the horse. Some made from a bridle or headstall that had left ridges on his face. Others on his neck and chest, even more on his legs. This horse had his own story.

At certain points, the man would ask the horse to move, doing so in a fluid, gentle manner, and the horse responded easily. Should the horse hesitate, the man spoke to him, as if to a puzzled child, and then the horse moved on as asked. The demonstration was short; the man thanked the horse, and then stepped from the pen.

Perhaps there were those there wondering just what that was all about? The man had not truly asked the horse to do anything, not anything in particular, nor did he instruct us as to how to do it. It was not, by any standard, much of a show. Perhaps there was more? Of course, there would be questions.

"What are you teaching him?" was the first one.

"He is teaching me. We are both learning," said the man. "The horse is our mirror. He shows us what we need to work on and he will respond to us."

"How long will that take?"

"It will never end, we will never be finished."

I looked up and the horse had returned to his spot to gaze down the river valley. He was totally ignoring us. I could see more scars, more of his story.

"This horse was given to me," told the man. "No one knew where he came from other than no one could ride him. He was sold to the rodeo as a bronco horse. They gave him to me because he became very dangerous, almost killed a man."

That got our attention. But before we were to get the story, the man started on his own story. "I was a bronco rider for many, many years. I followed the rodeo circuit, learning how to make a living riding, and roping, and working with tough, tough horses. I did that for forty years, ever since I was a young man. Then, one day, I saw what I was doing. It was not what The People had been taught for generation after generation; it was not in the interest of the horse. I decided that I needed to fix this, so I took horses people had no use for and gave them back their dignity. I discovered that first I had to learn how to do this; I had to return to the source of our teachings. I am here to tell you about it, not teach you, as many famous trainers do. You will need to find this within yourselves. Only then can you train a horse."

With that the demonstration ended, and we all went to dinner. The horse, I saw as I turned back for a last look, pinned his ears and threatened one of the guests who attempted to approach him. The man, with a soft cluck of his tongue, brought the horse back from the charge, placed his arm over his neck, and led him quietly from the pen.

Dinner chatter, of course, brought out comments about the afternoon's demonstration. "But he didn't DO anything," was one comment. Another, "I don't get what he is talking about, going back to the source. What source?" Some of the egos in the room were taking on some air, feeling safe to show off their expertise compared to the man's. We nodded at such comments but remained in the background, as did several other guests who were not at all horse literate, just friends of our hostess. Knowing that we could explain some of what they saw, they drew us aside.

"That was amazing," gushed one of the guests. She knew nothing of horses but she had grasped the message. "I could see how that horse treated him, with such respect and kindness. A horse that had the scars to prove that he had led a very different life." Good for her, I thought, at least someone here is "getting it."

After dinner, which was fabulous, our well-fed group was asked to go down to the river. Seats were set out alongside the strong current which faced us upstream, towards the fading light. Standing before us was the man, this time in full Native American regalia. How impressive. He used a small drum, and his chanting voice, to draw us into the story of The People. He bent to the earth, he pointed to the water, he raised his arms toward the sky; all the time telling how The People and nature and all animals had a strong bond that needed to be respected and nurtured so they could become one.

The stories, like Biblical parables, carried a message. The evening air was a refreshing welcome after a hot Montana afternoon, and the sky darkened into a cobalt blue before night would envelop us. Behind the man, a rainbow appeared, perhaps the result of a maverick rainstorm further up the valley, or perhaps conjured from his words. The group, even the skeptical ones, were drawn deeper into the story. Then, coming towards us on silent, outstretched wings, was a bald eagle. He came with the words of the man, circled us, dipping just low enough for us to hear the wind through his feathers; then he was gone.

We were one overwhelmed group of people that evening. No one was "not getting it." Even the egos. As we walked up to thank this man, this incredible man, we shared the experience of the rainbow and the eagle that had appeared behind him.

His response, "I am not surprised."

KHARIS

Cataplexy is a problematic and potentially dangerous aspect of narcolepsy. This fact will mean nothing to you until you finish the story.

—ᴍ—

The UPS man knocked on my door, "Did you know one of your horses is loose?"

"Yes, thank you for pointing that out," I said, "he has been loose for fifteen years. You must be new on this route."

Slightly embarrassed, he admitted he was.

"I should warn you about the goat then," I said, scouting the barn area to see if the goat had detected the UPS truck and was heading for yet another adventure of hopping inside and tossing packages about while the unsuspecting driver was busy at the door.

He thanked me for the warning and drove off wondering what he might find the next time he had a delivery to our farm. I hoped it would be the same, although I knew that the days of my roaming horse would come to an end, after all he was thirty-one years old.

Kharis was the progeny of two highly valued black Arabian horses; had he been born black, I would have never known him. The recessive color to black is bright, and I mean bright, chestnut, the color of a newly minted copper penny, almost orange. He was shuffled out the back gate as quickly as possible never to be seen by customers who sought out black horses. A friend took him home and raised him to be a particularly handsome young horse.

"How about training my horse for me," he asked one day. And that was our introduction.

In my lifetime, he was the easiest horse I ever trained. He had everything going for him, intelligence, athletic build, fabulous looks, everything but sturdy legs. Even at age four I could see he would be challenged to stay sound, so I passed on buying him. Two years later, in a weak moment, I bought him anyway. Perhaps the most emotionally driven purchase of my life, I have never regretted it.

Kharis, full name, Habibi Bukharis, which means "my darling Bukharis", lived up to his name. He taught everyone in our barn to ride and drive with the kindness of a governess. As predicted, his legs soon started to fail him and eventually he was retired. We moved to

Vermont where he was given the run of the place, a job he took very seriously, and he became a figure on the farm.

Having the freedom of say, a dog, is unusual for a horse. Kharis saw it as his duty to greet every visiting trailer and accompanied new horses to their stalls. There, he would stand all night and assure them that all was well. He was always there when horses were bathed or shod or the vet came for a visit. His steady demeanor calmed the twitchiest of horses as he whispered to them that this was a place where the grass was plentiful.

As the years went on, Kharis objected more and more about being confined, even if confinement meant closing him in a pasture. The barn, the yard were his. He would stand at the gate and whinny; if that did not work he tossed his head; and if that did not work he would stand right up on his hind legs. Even at age thirty-one, he could do that! We were especially careful about not locking him in.

Closed doors became an obsession with Kharis. He liked them open for no other apparent reason than he liked them open. Unused stalls were closed and latched, only to find them soon open thanks to the efforts of my old horse. When Lucky first arrived, he stayed in a stall for his first night, only to be found roaming the lawn with Kharis the next morning. Care had to be taken any time Lucky was stalled, as Kharis would spring him in no time flat if we forgot to place a snap on the latch. Only Lucky received this honor as all the other horses were left to spend the night quietly in their stalls.

I was particularly careful about the aging horse's health although he was remarkably free of any old horse ailments other than his creaky gait. At twenty-seven, my vet, Heather, and I decided that this would be, perhaps, the last time we dared tranquilize him for tooth care.

"I want to take a good look," she said, "in case he has any broken teeth or cavities." This being a routine procedure, neither one of us thought anything of it. We did not think Kharis would care either as he had witnessed countless veterinary procedures in the barn. His head was often right in there with ours during a procedure.

I grabbed a halter and started to walk towards him. Heather had drawn the drugs and was standing quietly in the barn aisle. As I approached Kharis, he suddenly realized that the halter was meant for him; and the syringe. His head went up as he started backwards; he took but two steps before completely collapsing into a pile on the floor. He hit his head against the wall on the way down.

I gasped.

Heather gasped.

For the first time ever, I saw her at a loss for words. A vet at a loss for words is not a common sight. She looked at me, looked at the syringe in her hand and said, "I didn't do it."

Horrified, we raced to the collapsed horse, who, to our relief, was starting to struggle back onto his feet, somewhat shaken, but fine.

"He fainted," whispered Heather. "I have never seen it, but I have heard of it."

We opted not to continue with his teeth exam.

Two times after that I witnessed Kharis' fainting syndrome. Once when a horse got loose and ran full tilt down the barn aisle past Kharis, the other when a storm blew up when Kharis was too far from the barn for shelter.

It is called cataplexy.

My old horse has it.

We do our best not to scare him.

JUST KIDDING

When most people think about getting a pet, they think dog, cat, rabbit, or hamster. Not Tim, he was thinking Scottish Highlander cow. His wife was thinking that this idea had better pass. Not that he could not keep a cow; they had a lovely, restored farmhouse with an ample bank barn and acres and acres of land. "I can just picture a cow out there," said Tim.

"Humph," said his wife.

Even after acquiring two horses and two more boarded horses, Tim was still not satisfied. He wanted a cow. Not just any cow; a Scottish Highlander, a rare breed that looked like they just melted out of the ice, with a huge, hairy head and long, long horns. "I think they are pretty," said Tim.

"Humph," said his wife.

I was taking advantage of the longer light of late spring to weed the flowerbeds when Tim brought up the question, "What do you think about having a pet cow?" Why he would ask someone who raised baby goats in the house, shared a laundry room with a pair of raccoons, and had a free-range horse on the lawn, about rationalizing a cow was beyond me. I liked cows, but was obviously a goat person, given that my two pet goats were nibbling up the weeds I was pulling as I worked. Why they could not pull up the weeds themselves was a question, but they seemed to like most of what I offered them.

"My wife is not keen on the idea," he said. "She thinks having two Bernese Mountain dogs in the house is OK, but I can't have a cow in the barn? Those dogs are the size of small ponies."

"Perhaps you should get a pony?" I suggested, pulling a valued flower from the lips of Margaret. Margaret was only three months old and just learning about flowers; I still had hopes of influencing her taste. I had a fifty/fifty chance of that being successful.

"I really want a cow."

Tim was killing time with me while his wife, along with several other members of our foxhunt, were having a staff meeting in the house. His wife was a lovely lady with a great sense of humor and a good friend of mine. She also kept a spotless house, garden and barn. I was thinking a cow might hamper that.

Innocently, I said, "How about a goat?"

"I don't know much about goats, are they as nice as cows?"

Did he not notice the two goats sniffing along the dirt with me, playfully pulling on my sleeve and dancing around in circles, enticing me to play with them? The larger, older goat, Nudge, was a Cashmere, and Margaret was a Boer kid. Both had floppy ears, full bodies and pleasant dispositions. Both were happy to play with anyone who would engage them. Both were pretty darn spoiled when it came to being a goat.

"Nicer," I replied, "you can play with a goat. It might be a bit dangerous to play with a Scottish Highlander cow."

This got Tim thinking. He picked up my instructions on goat behavior and goat play very quickly. He was really getting into it when the meeting broke up, and our guests, including his wife, filed out onto the lawn. Thinking he would have some fun with her, he approached her with the goat.

"Hi honey, so, instead of getting cow, how about a goat?"

"What?"

"See this goat, Sue will give her to me."

"What!?"

"I can take her home with us, tonight, what do you think?"

What she thought was that Tim was playing a frightfully good practical joke on her and waiting to see how she reacted. Regaining her composure, she gave a little laugh and said, "Sure, honey, let's go," and she started for the car.

Not wanting to miss any of this, the rest of the group gathered closer in order to join in the fun.

"I'm serious," returned Tim, "she would be easier than a cow."

"You want a cow?" asked a member of the group.

"To eat?" asked another.

"No, no," Tim gasped, "as a pet."

"A pet cow?"

"See, see," quipped his wife, "they don't think it's a good idea either."

"What kind of cow?"

"A Scottish Highlander."

"Whoa, wait a minute here," a comment coming quickly from Tim's veterinarian. "You want the cow that looks like they just melted out of the ice with the huge hairy head and long, long horns?"

"Yes, those are the ones, I think they are pretty."

"I will say this," said the veterinarian as she turned directly to his wife. "Let him have the goat if you want to keep me as your vet."

"But.. but, we are not getting a cow or a goat."

"See honey, our vet thinks it is a good idea."

"What?!"

"Oh, she's so cute," chimed another member of the group, "what's her name?"

"Margaret."

"Your horses will love her," commented another, "goats and horses make great companions."

Wondering if this was one incredibly well played out practical joke, or that she was actually going to put a three month old goat into the back of their Lincoln Navigator and take her home, his wife started to panic. "No, no, no, we are not getting a cow and we are not getting a goat."

But the group was having too much fun with this. Tim was getting goat care instructions from the vet as the husband was digging out a nice blanket for Margaret to sit on for her ride home. Buoyed by such support, Tim was determined to have his pet. I sealed the deal with a guaranteed return should things not work out.

Defeated, his wife turned to Tim and said; "You do realize that I may not speak to you for a long, long time."

"I understand."

"And that goat sits in back."

"I understand."

Climbing into the back seat, with a smile from ear to ear, went Tim and his new goat, Margaret. We laughed and cheered as they drove off, everyone thinking that the goat would surely come back.

She did not.

And wasn't she on their Christmas card that December?!

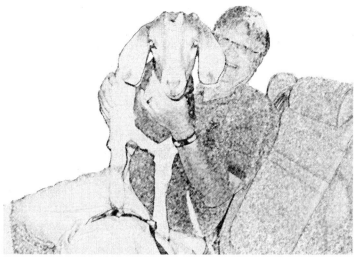

COACHING IN BAVARIA

The Maypoles in the center of each village stood as symbols of the rural Bavarian culture of nestled villages in the surrounding farmland. Our view of the countryside was from the top of a century old Road Coach pulled by four brawny Hanoverian stallions. As guests of Andreas Nemitz' "Coaching in Bavaria," we were on a three-day tour of the region between Lake Starnberg and Lake Ammersee and Neuschwanstein Castle. Two other guests shared the coach with us allowing us more room and freedom than usual on such a tour. This was the husband's idea of the perfect vacation.

While most tourists sightsee from a car or bus, we had opted for horse and carriage. This was not just any carriage; it was a Road Coach. The kind of carriage one sees in old prints that carried twelve people and were, during the 1800's, the public mode of transportation in Europe and Great Britain. Too heavy for American travel, they were replaced by the Concord Stage Coach which served the same purpose of connecting passengers to trains and steamboats in this country.

Our itinerary promised not just the beautiful scenery of Bavaria, but a chance to slip back in time to travel old coaching routes, lunch at brae houses and stay in century old inns. We started out on the old Roman Road, the "Via Claudia Augusta" to drive through the small town of Saulgrub. Then we reached the so-called "King's Road", where King Ludwig II used to hasten from one castle to the other, mostly after midnight. King Ludwig had developed severe paranoia in his later years that kept his travels cloaked in darkness.

The "roads" were remarkably close to being what they were centuries earlier. They tracked through stretches of the forest where tiny chapels, tucked into the woods, were bright with ribbons and flowers. Our pace, about five miles an hour, allowed for far more detailed observation than in a bus or car.

The Road Coach was authentic, having been restored to continue the rigors of travel, but still kept its original design. A driver sat on the top of the carriage on the front right hand seat, also called the box seat, where he controlled the four horses through two sets of reins, four reins in all, which he held in his left hand. His right hand made adjustments to the reins whenever necessary. There was a seat next to him on which we were invited to sit should we wish so. Behind him was a seat that would hold four passengers and back-to-back from that was another seat for four passengers who would face the rear of the coach. The last seat held four more people facing forward, one of whom traditionally was the guard or groom. Inside the coach were places for four people. Four not so big people who sat shoulder to shoulder, knee to knee, facing each other. A century earlier these were the first-class seats as they offered shelter from the elements, which the roof seats did not.

Reliving that experience gave one a healthy appreciation of the people, and horses, of the 1800's. Should a passenger in one of the roof seats doze off, he stood a strong chance of being bounced to the ground, hence the saying " to drop off to sleep." Speed and reliability was the root of the Road Coach names. "Arrow," "Rocket," "Dart," and "Comet." Hunt country had coaches such as "Tally-Ho", "Nimrod," and "Hark Away."

I tried to envision myself stuffed into one of the inside seats for four-hour intervals wearing a full-length dress and corset while bouncing along on dirt roads. Stops to change horses offered the only opportunity to disembark and take care of one's needs. I am sure that the full length dress added some frustration to that process. The coaching runs held to a strict time schedule with pride being taken in how quickly a change of horses took place. I had to wonder how the ladies did it!

Because we had driving experience, we actually owned and drove a vehicle similar to this, we were invited to help. The husband could not have been happier when he was offered the reins. This allowed the coachman to expound on the history of the areas through which we were passing. We stopped at a lovely private home for lunch and toured their family chapel on the grounds. We continued on to a small village where we stayed at a jolly old inn complete with a beer hall and creaky wooden floors. We were having a grand time.

The second day was as grand as the first. But the third morning was grey; the forecast predicted a light rain. I was accustomed to rain as I was known to be a magnet for such weather. Once, when I arrived in Dubai at the edge of the Arabian Desert, it rained for the first time in five years. The husband knew right away that I was the reason he was about to get wet. It was not as if I liked getting wet either, rain just seemed to follow me. We were supplied with excellent wax cloth blankets to place over our laps, and we forgave the light drizzle as it did not hinder the enjoyment of

our travel. However, the other two guests opted for the shelter inside of the coach. We now had the top of the coach to ourselves!

By this point, the husband had struck up quite a friendship with the driver and the two discussed coach driving in detail. He was truly having a fabulous time. When we arrived at a short, but fairly steep hill, the husband was invited to place the skid under the coach's rear wheel. Brakes existed, but were designed to slow the coach, not actually hold it back on a hill. Instead, a metal skid attached to a heavy chain, was placed under one rear wheel which stopped the wheel completely and allowed it to slide down the hill, friction being the brake. Using the skid brought us even closer to the historic experience we were having.

However, the increasing rain was also giving us the feel of travel over one hundred years ago. No windshield wipers; no windshield, no roof! We hunkered into our oil cloths still determined to get the full experience of coach travel. The other two guests peered out from their snug inside seats and had to wonder just what was wrong with us. But from the inside, one saw very little of Bavaria and missed the feel of the four noble horses that were drawing us. We got wet, but it was August, and although not that warm, and we still were having an enjoyable time.

Around noon, we arrived at the Wies Church, the most beautiful rococo church in Germany. Here, we disembarked and went into the warm tavern for a hot lunch and delicious beer with lemonade. The rain pounded at the windows as we peered out to the parking lot where bus after bus of tourists arrived to see the church. It took some inner strength to leave the tavern and rejoin our driver and coach to continue our journey. We noted that our two other guests had abandoned the trip for a cozy night at the Inn and a motor ride to our final destination. Not us, we were there for the full experience!

The moment we reached our seats on top of the coach we realized that the oil cloths were soaked through. Having been used to protect the horses while we ate lunch, they had reached their limit of water resistance and lay on our laps like heavy, wet dogs. Only the difference being that dogs had personality and warmth; these did not.

I was beginning to remember why I disliked getting soaked and wondered about the wisdom of continuing on. As we passed through the herd of busses in the parking lot, we found ourselves the same height as those sitting inside their cozy, warm, dry busses. We must have seemed like an illusion, for we glided by with no obvious source of locomotion as the horses and coach were lower and out of view. The tourists gaped, rising from their seats, to see just what we were all about.

Eye to eye with our new friends, we became acutely conscious of our physical appearance. Drooping hats were drawn down to protect our faces from the rain, and cloaked in huge sagging oilcloth drapes; we must have looked pretty pathetic. Apparently not so. The awe in the faces of those tourists reminded us of how distinctive our transport was for surely they had never thought such a thing existed. Like royalty, we appeared to have such a conveyance, a coach drawn by four horses, like Cinderella or Queen Elizabeth of England. Anybody could get a seat on a bus, but how to get a seat on that coach? Buoyed by our newfound fame, we straightened up, lifted our chins and gave them a polite little Queen Victoria wave back. Despite our drowned appearance, we were envied in their eyes.

After lunch, we drove through lonely mountain forests and across pastures with grazing herds of cattle. We stopped on occasion to open and close a field gate. We come to the lakes of Forggensee and Bannwaldsee with both the royal castles, Neuschwanstein and Hohenschwangau, in close proximity. Neuschwanstein, the fairy castle in the clouds from which Disneyland modeled Sleeping Beauty's castle and Hohenschwangau at Swan Lake, the picturesque childhood home of King Ludwig II. With both castles towering high above our coach, they peeped through the overcast skies as if they were playing hide and go seek with us. We would get a glimpse of a white tower, unattached to anything, floating in the clouds like an apparition. It would soon disappear and another piece of a castle would emerge from the mist.

The rain had made the going slow for the horses, so we were on route an extra hour or so. Around dinner time, we arrived at our hotel. We stepped off the coach soaked and chilled to the bone, looking forward to the comfort of a warm room and a pleasant dinner. Our luggage was slid out from under more soaked oilcloths and did not look much better than we did. We bade goodbye to our coachman and patted those magnificent horses for our safe passage and turned towards the anticipated warmth of a dry, cozy room.

We could not get our wet clothes off fast enough and soon discovered that our room was not much warmer than the chilly day outside. The hotel saw no need for heat in August. Desperate, I turned to the bathroom and started filling the tub with hot water. We huddled in towels until we could slip our feet into the warmth and slowly, together, submerged ourselves up to our necks. We were ever so thankful for large, deep, European tubs.

We soon discovered that the towels we had wrapped around us were the only dry garments we had. Our luggage had suffered, in its position on top of the coach, the same fate as the oil cloths. Just about everything was damp, if not just downright wet. Putting those wet clothes back on was one of the hardest things we have ever done but we were soon rewarded with a fire near our table in the dining room. We must have appeared a bit odd in that we kept switching our chairs to get all of our clothing dry. We felt, indeed, like travelers of a century earlier, having to be resourceful, and not too fussy, about what a day's adventures would bring.

ALARMED

Without a doubt, my crow, Alfie, was the reason I managed to get a college degree.

At this time in my life, I was living at home and commuting to Rutgers University, which perhaps is the root of my life's desire never again to be stuck in traffic. What should have been a twenty-minute drive turned into an hour of stop-and-go traffic thanks to every car in New Jersey being on the road at the same time every morning. Needless to say, an eight o'clock class was murder.

Eight o'clock classes meant getting up at five in order to feed the horses, change clothes, drive, locate a parking spot in some remote lot and hike to class. I tried taking the park and ride bus, but I missed them more often than not, which made me repeatedly late for class. This became exceedingly tiresome, so I started developing ways to shave off a minute here and a minute there.

I decided to skip changing my clothes from the barn after feeding my horses in the morning. I was an Ag. Major and in barns at school anyway, so what if I got odd looks in English class? I researched every route to school, the back roads actually offering ten minutes less of driving time. I knew every traffic light, how many times it changed before I finally drove through said traffic light, as well as becoming an expert at parallel parking my car where no one else dared. Half of my studying time occurred in my car, with my notes on the dash, so I could review them while waiting out a traffic light.

All of my manipulations, however, did not improve my attendance record. Whatever time I had squeezed out of the commute was converted to sleep-in time in the morning. My biological clock was not set for early mornings. No matter how hard I tried to discipline myself, my ability to sleep through an alarm clock was remarkable. There was not an alarm clock made that I could not outwit.

Then I acquired Alfie.

One does not acquire a crow that easily. This particular crow had misfiled his flight plan, and that resulted in a broken wing, a benevolent bystander, and a visit to the vet. My willingness to adopt any creature in need was common knowledge, and the vet knew my phone number by heart!

Alfie understood his plight beyond what any wild creature should have. He accepted human help without panic, without fear, without hostility. Despite our efforts, the wing did not heal well enough to allow for sustainable flight, and Alfie was grounded forever. He did not seem to mind.

Alfie shared my room on the third floor of my father's house. It was a renovated attic which I loved as it gave me both space and privacy and a terrific view of the backyard. Growing just as tall as the house was an old apple tree, one that I had climbed many summer days as a child. The branches were still worn smooth from my childhood grip, and it stood as a welcome old friend just outside of my window. Which was, also, Alfie's window.

Jammed against the window screen, his cage was but a few feet from the nearest branch of the apple tree and another world. In one direction from his cage was my attic room that offered shelter and food. But in the other direction were wind and rain, birds and squirrels, and all of the scents and sensations a wild bird was attuned to. Alfie made an admirable blend of his two worlds and managed to fit into both.

Crows greet each other with a big, healthy "CAW!" Me included. I would not quite have reached the front door of the house open when I heard the greeting from three stories above, "CAW!" Not content with a "Hi, Alfie" response, he would continue until I "CAWed!" back. A lot like a Tarzan movie, we worked out a dialog, somewhat limited in vocabulary, but a dialog nonetheless.

"CAW!"

"CAW!" said I.

"Caw"

"Caw back, be right up."

"Rrrrrrruppp!"

My father, not a man who ever spent much time with animals, and one who wondered how he spawned a daughter who had conversations with them, truly got into the "CAW" thing. I caught him coming through the door "cawing" when he did not expect me at home. Regular visitors also got into "cawing" as there was no relief until one answered, conversations being quite difficult under such circumstances.

Having trained me to greet him, Alfie tutored me further on crow-speak. He taught me that even with a limited vocabulary, one could communicate. Imagine having but one word, "HA", with which to express yourself. "Ha!" (pretty funny!). "Ha," (ah, I get it). "Ha." (gotcha). "Caw" had that many times ten meanings in which Alfie instructed me.

Spending his daylight hours at his window, he was well aware of what was going on in the bird world from his exposure to the many wild creatures that visited the top of that old apple tree. His visitors surely found it odd that he could not come out, but they spent time with Alfie anyway which, I am sure, helped him considerably in dealing with his captivity.

I was soon to learn the "grateful dance" when a bird was offered food. Fresh meat was always greeted with a quick gulp and a gesture for more, but once the initial feeding frenzy was over, Alfie would bow his head and purr, "rrrrrrrupppp - thank you."

Alfie ate raw meat and fruit with no special favorites. He got breakfast and dinner, as my college schedule did not allow for much more. I soon discovered that any food he could not eat he would wrap up in newspaper, from his bedding, and stick in the bars of the cage facing the window. Should he get hungry during the day, he could retrieve a tidbit, unwrap it and have a pleasant little snack. I had to be careful not to overfeed him, as the wrapped up balls would accumulate, and decompose, to the point that my father would notice a foul odor whiffing down the prevailing winds from my window to his.

Intrigued by crow behavior, I dove into the Rutgers Ag Library to learn as much as I could about crows. There was a lot about how to get rid of crows, everything from timed explosions to picking them off with a gun. Crows, historically, were not terribly helpful to man. Finally, I found a published research paper on crow behavior and sat down to several hours of fascinating reading. Alfie obviously had collaborated on this paper!

Our most out of the ordinary, and intimate, communication was in the spring. No doubt the birds in the old apple tree heralded the breeding season and Alfie caught right on. I was the only "girlfriend" he had and so he took to courting me. Always his free time in my room was supervised for fear that my pet rats might get the bad end of Alfie's exercise time. They peered with wonder from their little cages as Alfie hopped and flapped around the large room. Well, the flapping was pretty sad considering his damaged wing, but he never gave that up.

Starting with a series of "rrrruppps", Alfie hopped onto my hand and started a little dance. Gently taking a finger in his beak, he "rrru-upppped" and hopped and shuffled his feathers in a most delicate and entertaining way. He would repeat this courting dance every chance he had. He would even offer me food that he had put aside to take the opportunity to tell me what a lovely hand I had. Would I consider starting a nest with him? At times, it was a bit embarrassing!

I communicated the fact that my hand was dating a crow to one of my professors at school, and received a raised eyebrow in response.

"Imagine," he said, "if that got around campus!" He really was very interested so I kept notes of the events up on the third floor of my father's house. I suppose my failure to build a nest was enough for Alfie to give up on me but he repeated the courtship every spring for three years. We had a seasonal relationship.

I later learned of an owl that performed the mating ritual with his handler's hand and felt camaraderie with her that few people could share.

Back to the alarm clock and getting to class on time. I had one of those electric ones that buzzed. It had a nice set of buttons on top marked "on", "off", and "snooze." I knew those buttons by heart and could tap them from a semi-comatose state to snatch a "few" more minutes of precious sleep. In other words, I rarely made it to class on time. My sheepish appearance at class was getting old for my professors, and I was dangling my grades over the great abyss of failure.

Then, one early dawn when, after hitting all of the buttons with no result, I pulled the cord out of the wall in desperation to stop the noise.

"Buzzzzzzzz!"

Staring blankly at the pulled cord, buzzing continuing in my ears, I searched my sleepy brain for the source of the noise. The sound, coming from the direction of the window, was from my crow who was buzzing gleefully away.

"Stop!" I said.

"Caw?" he responded, all happy to see me up and available to feed him breakfast.

However, it did not take long for me to ignore not only the buzzing alarm clock, but also the buzzing crow.

In this seemingly hopeless state, I would never get through college. I launched a search for the most obnoxious alarm clock I could find. I tested countless at stores, annoying plenty of clerks as I did. I finally obtained a clock with a bell clangor with the voice of Hades, "Clannnngggggg!!!!!" I bolted straight out of bed that first morning, and Alfie hit the side of his cage with his beak in alarm.

It did not last. I surprised myself in my ability to find that clock with my hand, turn it off and still remain asleep.

But the crow would figure it out.

"Clannnngggggg!!!"

Ah! I cried, as I slapped the clock, until I realized that the sound was ticket to breakfast, and that alarm clock was the ticket to me. I could turn off the clock, but the crow kept it up until his little beak was busy with food and by that time, I was totally awake. Even if I did not set the alarm, the crow would go off, "clannnnnggggg!" at dawn. I was utterly outwitted.

Alfie got me to class for four years of college and proved to be a veritable feathered friend.

BICYCLE DRESSAGE

Early European aristocrats trained their horses to perform various maneuvers to assist their performance while in battle. From that came dressage – A French term, translated to mean "training". In modern dressage competition, training is demonstrated through the performance of "tests" of prescribed series of movements within a standard arena. Judges evaluate each movement with a score from zero to ten - zero being "not executed" and 10 being "excellent". Dressage is occasionally referred to as "Horse Ballet" and can be likened to figure skating.

Admittedly, it can be rather boring to watch. Howard Cosell, while acting as commentator for the Olympics, said, "It is a lot like watching paint dry." Unless one is really "into" the sport, dressage lacks the equine drama of show jumping or horse racing. The concept of bicycle dressage came from a group of very tired dressage judges who were unwinding after a long day of watching test after test after test. During a late dinner, the group got a bit silly. The conclusion they came up with that evening was that dressage was a concept; therefore, it could be performed with anything, not just a horse. After running through numerous examples, such as figure skating was "dressage on ice" and dog obedience was "dressage with a dog", they came up with the idea of doing dressage with a bicycle. They forgot all about it the next morning.

Seven years later, I came across notes and diagrams that had been worked painstakingly out that evening on a napkin. I shared this with a friend who was quick to see a good thing and immediately set to work to initiate the very first Bicycle Dressage competition, ever.

Saratoga Springs was famous for many reasons, one of which is its extensive exhibition of the best dressage horses in the country over Memorial Day weekend. The event we were involved with was driven dressage, one done with a horse and carriage. Included in the program, for the very first time, was Bicycle Dressage. It had been designed to follow the American Driving Society's Preliminary short test. The rationale of using a driving test was that it had something to do with wheels. We were amazed to get four genuine responses to the concept. "Just what is this and how do we enter?" they asked. We were in trouble.

Looking to the fellow "originators" of the concept, we asked, "What rules should we have?"

The joint response was "As long as they are peddling something, there are no rules." Imagine that; a sport with no rules. It was bound to catch on.

The day of the competition there were some decidedly serious looking bicycle riders warming up by the ring. The show stopped, and the driving competitors were treated to some remarkably innovative interpretations of "dressage."

The first competitor was a dressage rider as well as a carriage driver. Fully clad in top hat and tails and a set of sky blue spandex tights, she peddled in the arena, saluted and rode her test with extreme accuracy and conviction. The next rider was her husband, this being his debut of entering any form of a dressage arena. "He has refused to ride or drive our horses in a show, but jumped at the chance of "showing" his bicycle," commented his wife. He did a very good test, remarking to his wife later that dressage was harder than he thought it would be. She smiled the rest of the day.

The next entrant was somewhat intimidated by the first two performances. "I was worried," he commented, "they obviously practiced." But, by performing a flying dismount from his bicycle for the walk section he got the judges' attention. He saluted at the end, bent down, folded up the bicycle, and left with it slung over his shoulder. He got a round of applause from the increasing number of on-lookers.

I, however, had the winning test. Clad totally in pink and riding a pink bicycle (with Barbie streamers, no less) I stunned the judges with my ability to chew gum and ride a bike at the same time. "When she popped that last bubble in time with her halt, she had my vote", admitted judge Craig Kellogg. I took my victory round ringing my Barbie bell and popped a bubble full in the face. My comment after the test was, "Warming up the gum so that it was just right for bubbles was the hardest part."

Bicycle Dressage was on its way. The next event was held in conjunction with the Green Mountain Horse Association combined driving event in Vermont. This time, however, there was a celebrity jury of judges. David Sanders, who had spent many years as Prince Phillip's groom and navigator, thought the entire event "most bully." "This would catch on like crazy back in Britain." Hopeton Kimball, who exemplifies the qualities of a gentile lady, will be forever remembered for her uncontrolled giggles.

Originality being the cornerstone of the sport, entrants came up with skillful tests. The first was a paux de dieu by Lana Wright, a former Olympian, and her daughter. Their timing was excellent with an interesting interpretation of "the lengthened pedal across the diagonal". They were followed by a second paux de dieu made up of two very talented bicyclists that had not a clue about dressage. But as originally noted by the founders, dressage is a concept, and they performed an excellent test.

The next entry was a tandem bicycle. The "driver" was clad in formal attire with his "proper" groom behind. Unfortunately, it was a vintage bike and the chain jumped the track during the sixth movement. The bike faltered, then dropped the ground, with pleading cries from the entrant of "mechanic, mechanic, please help my bike, it needs a mechanic." Unfortunately for the bike, the only "medical staff" at the event was a veterinarian. He knew nothing about bikes, and was forced to declare that the bike was done.

The hands down winners in Vermont had built up their routine since the Saratoga event. Jeff and Tiny Rubenstein entered the ring on a tandem bike, dressed in top hats, tails and "Mickey Mouse" white gloves. They synchronized their salutes, halts, dismounts and walk with amazing precision and showmanship, earning the respect of not only the jury of judges, but also that of the crowd.

"The only sad part about the whole thing was that it was over," the winners remarked. "Practicing and working up a bicycle routine was oodles more fun than getting a horse ready for dressage."

The only thing left to make this sport even more fun would be to have the horses judge the bicycle riders!

CROSSING THE STREAM

The horse took in the air with his nostrils and knew immediately he was home. Before I could unload him from the trailer, he had whinnied his arrival and had heard the familiar return from his sister. He passed from my hands with hardly a notice, and I felt a twinge of betrayal from the horse with whom I had been so close for nearly a year. That year had transposed him from a suffering, dangerous horse into the magnificent animal he was that day. Would he know me a year from now? Would he remember our journey, as I always will? Perhaps it would be better for him to leave all of that behind and get on with life, but I could not help but to hope that he would keep a special place for me in his soul.

It is not fortuitous to name an animal "Lucky", an acumen pointed out when the bay Morgan colt was foaled. The name was his regardless which is why he has a story. It started as a bright day that offered the opportunity for a pleasant ride. Lucky was four months old and accustomed to following his mother for such events. He was playful, as all colts are, and enjoyed frolicking off to explore his new world before rushing back to the security of his mother's side. All but this one time he had been safe. He did not see the old fence wire strung at the edge of the field. No one had seen it; no one had ever known it was there. He hit it innocently. He hit it so hard it flipped him over, caught his hind leg, and dangled him like a hare in a wire trap.

The mare sensed his absence; the riders turned back to witness his plight. They could do nothing. One rider raced back to the barn for tools and help, while the other stayed to reassure him, comfort him, beg him not to fight and make it worse. He took that advice and hung there for a long time. Help came; he was cut down and lay quietly before gaining his legs again. A bit wobbly, but able to follow his mother home, he appeared unscathed, but he would never be the same again.

The differences in Lucky were subtle at first. His right shoulder was developing more than his left. His gait was a bit ungainly. He carried his head to one side. By the time Lucky was four, he had grown accustomed to compensating for his damaged body and was actually performing nicely in his training as a riding and driving horse. Sure there were a few issues, but he was young and that was to be expected. Except instead of growing out of some of his coltish habits, the habits grew with him. Everyone had noticed that his back was not straight, it "corkscrewed", but no one, including his vet, seemed to think it bothered him. He had tried to tell them, the grooms, and his rider, that the increasing demands of his training were causing discomfort. He started by swishing his tail, then stomping his right hind foot, then pinning his ears. By the time I saw him that summer, he had charged the grooms when they attempted to collect him from the pasture, was disagreeable to load on the trailer, and had scared off the veterinary chiropractor. By the time I saw him that summer; he was completely out of control.

What does it mean when a horse is out of control? Lots of movie scenes give a fair representation with horses baring their teeth, rearing, striking, and running around tossing their manes and pounding the dirt. Lucky could have been cast in such a role. Perhaps not as dramatic as the movies, but he was still pretty darn impressive.

What on earth happened to this nice, well cared for horse? I was shocked. The grooms were terrified. His owner was in tears. Any other horse, in such a situation, would have been labeled a rogue. Such a beautiful animal deserved the chance to figure out what was wrong, and Lucky got that chance when I, somewhat naively, offered to take him home and try to work things out. The husband shot me one of those "oh, no," glances but I knew he would be supportive. He always was.

I was not about to take this horse on alone. I had the advantage of having my good friend, Heather, as my vet, and one of the best horse massage therapists in New England, Norm, as part of my team. We had worked on several other "bad boys" in the past with excellent results. We were not natural horsemanship gurus or wild bronco tamers; rather, we bounced ideas around between us and worked out veterinary and behavior techniques as we went. I truly enjoyed working with these two talented people, and I knew they would accept this new challenge with vigor.

"Are you crazy?" Heather said when she first saw Lucky. Her remark came right after he pinned his ears and snapped at my arm, a near miss. Both of us had whips in hand and did not dare take our eyes off of him as we deliberated how to start treatment.

The entire stance of the horse was tense and uncomfortable, and just the suggestion of touch set him off. "Leave me alone," he shouted at us, putting his wordless vocabulary into gestures. We both understood the message and were failing miserably in convincing him that our intent was to help, not hurt. Heather did manage to manipulate his hip, which pleased him so much he kicked out. "I can't imagine putting an acupuncture needle into this horse, although it would help him a great deal," she said. "In fact, I don't think I will ever be doing acupuncture on this horse." Heather was trying to tell me that perhaps I had taken on a lost cause.

"He gets a chance," I countered. "He does not have another option."

"OK," she said. "I just hope his name saves him."

I turned to Lucky, stared him straight in the eye, and said, "No other option, do you understand, work with us, or your life is over." Harsh words; but the truth.

Norm heard my warning that Lucky was "a bit of a handful", and haphazardly ignored it. Before Lucky could react, Norm was touching his neck and working the magic of his trade, and, perhaps for the first time in years, human touch felt good to him. Lucky was so surprised that he accepted Norm's talented touch, which gave us that first "crack in the armor" that we needed to get down to the real issues.

Week after week there were small, but appreciative, improvements. However, the swishing tail, kicking hind legs, and occasional snap of the jaws continued. He never gave us a warning before he blew; it came swift as a snake. I had made the assumption that Lucky had come to respect me and knew the consequences if he did not. How dumb was I? With Norm waiting in the barn, I walked into the pasture to catch him; he charged me, mouth open, ears pinned, malice in his eyes.

A horse had not charged me in a long, long time. It is one hair-raising experience. While instinct might say, "run", experience says not. No way am I going to outrun a horse. I have learned a great deal from observing horses. Aggression only works if there is a reaction. It is kind of like playing "chicken," whoever backs down first is the loser. I charged back.

I heard Norm, who was standing at the fence, take in a gasp of air. Lucky, completely disarmed by my aggressive behavior, leapt to the side and offered a half hearted kick before running for the cover of the barn. I was so furious with him that I raced after him and cornered him in the stall where I gave him a full dose of verbal abuse, never touching him, but threatening with voice and stature. He stood stock-still. So did Norm! "I see what you mean," he stammered, "he is a bit dangerous!"

The charging incident did not do a lot for Lucky's future. I did not dismiss the concerns of my colleagues or the other option. I still felt we had yet to discover the reason for his behavior and was reluctant to quit just yet.

"No guarantees," I told his owner. "But I appreciate your giving me some time to work this out." Time was Lucky's enemy; he did not have much left.

Heather sensed the urgency of the situation and stepped back to study her patient. We could see what was wrong, but the cause remained hidden. The overdeveloped shoulder, the crooked back, the way he stood, the way he carried his neck, all just a hair wrong for what a healthy four-year-old horse should look like. What was it? On a hunch, Heather took a pen and poked Lucky on his left ribcage. Nothing. She poked harder. Nothing. Finally, she took out a hypodermic needle and tapped him all across his left side. Nothing! Lucky had no feeling on his left side! Working from areas where he did have feeling, Heather mapped out the "dead" area, which was considerable, and stepped back.

"I've never seen anything like this," she commented, "never even heard of such a thing. It does explain why everything else in his body is out of normal range as he has been compensating for this for four years. The question is, how to treat it?"

We both knew that answer, acupuncture, to the horse she had sworn she was never going to place a needle into. "He has to behave a lot better before I even dare try it," she said, opening the path to what we hoped would be Lucky's salvation.

I was truly struggling with how to get Lucky to the turning point, after which treatment could continue. Even with daily lessons, given any opportunity, he was still willing to challenge us. Any moment I was off guard Lucky took advantage. I was as quick and hard on him as possible, yet his reaction was only to back off, not accept.

A call to a horse psychic turned out to be the best decision I made with this horse. "Turn him out with the herd," she said, "give him some perspective." I had five horses that lived together in an especially happy herd situation. Everyone knew their place and was comfortable with that. None were aggressive-none were nasty.

What they taught him in three days, I could not have done in a year. He quickly learned that ignoring a warning sign meant serious consequences. He learned to wait his turn going through a gate, to respect the space of others and, if he charged anyone, I am sure he got what he deserved. By the third day, I was looking at a decidedly different horse!

I must admit it took some nerve to walk out into the pasture to collect Lucky from the herd. I banked on the other horses having taught him that aggressive behavior was not tolerated, and that if he charged me, it would be treated as a transgression to the herd. Lucky was singularly unsure of my approach; his ears flicked forward, then back, then forward, but he dared not move. For the first time, I caught him without using a whip, placing my hand on his neck and then sliding on the halter. Lucky walked quietly to the barn with me, again, the herd influence overriding any interest he might have had at balking or fighting.

From that point on, Lucky improved in leaps and bounds. I no longer needed a whip to lead him. I could work around him without worry that he would bite or kick. He accepted the acupuncture and was considerably more relaxed with the chiropractic sessions. He, in fact, fell asleep during one of Norm's massages!

We all knew that there was a long way to go before Lucky's future could be secure. Could he sustain a reasonable amount of work without the pain returning? How much of the nerve damage could be recovered? Would he continue to behave once back at home? As Norm so aptly put it, "Working on Lucky was like peeling an onion. Each time I got through a layer there was another one to deal with." Our work had just begun.

As all of this was transpiring, Lucky developed a lump on his neck. It was not painful but would not go away even with hot compresses and ice. It slowly, but steadily, grew over the weeks until it was of considerable size, yet it still did not seem to hurt him. Heather finally decided to lance it. A staggering amount of pus came forth. It appeared to be a sterile abscess that surrounded some foreign material that had worked into his neck. It could have been in there a long, long time; or perhaps it was a poison coming out, releasing Lucky from his aggressive behavior.

Now that the pain was under control, Lucky's body was rearranging itself. In addition to the acupuncture, we applied an electromagnetic blanket every day. The energy field stimulated his muscles and increased circulation. We hoped that stimulation to the "dead" area would help reconnect Lucky with that part of his body that he had not ever known. We watched, like excited children, for any sign of muscle activity.

Lucky's body rewarded us every time he had acupuncture. As the first needle was placed, all of the acupuncture points along that meridian responded creating a line of dots along his spine, over his croup and down his hindquarters. At first it was just one meridian, but as the months passed by, four meridians would "light up" as well as those down to his girth. Heather took pictures, as it was so unique a response. Although not as dramatic, Lucky would "light up" for Norm during a massage, a true indication that his body was responding to touch and healing. It was very, very rewarding for us.

Perhaps the most dramatic physical change was Lucky's mane.

Morgans are known for their flowing manes, but Lucky's was exceptional. It was thick and long and flowed beautifully from his arched neck making him quite the handsome horse. It had, for four years, hung off the right side of his neck. Three months into Lucky's treatment his mane started its migration to the left side. It started slowly, a wisp of hair over the withers, not uncommon, but followed by more and more until half was on one side and half on the other.

The moving mane was splendid news, indeed. It meant that Lucky's body carriage had changed enough to shift his neck position. His bulging left ribcage, unable to move correctly, had caused his neck to compensate by hanging off to the right. However, as our treatment slowly woke up the nerves on his left side and the rib cage was starting to respond, Lucky's neck was coming back to the center of this body. Such movement was ever so slight, but on a thousand pound animal, a fraction of an inch of change in one part of the body was reflected throughout. Lucky's mane was indicative of his body returning to normal position.

Perhaps Lucky's name was going to save him after all.

Vermont offered a rare treat; early spring. With it came the opportunity to resume Lucky's training as a riding and driving horse. I decided to take the approach of starting at the very beginning, as if he were an unbroken horse. Our first session, simply putting a bit in his mouth, proved so traumatic for Lucky it stunned me. Lucky continued to behave as if he had never had any training, and he continued to act surprised, and somewhat objectionable, at each step of the process. He was tense, challenging and at times defiant to the simplest requests from me. I took a step back.

Why was this his reaction? He had been ridden and driven before, yet showed little to no connection to understanding what I was asking of him. He balked at walking out the back driveway, he refused to stand for more than ten seconds, and he was acting like a horse with no training at all. Why?

Whenever I get stumped with a horse, I try to think like that horse. Lucky had submitted to being ridden and driven in spite of his physical issues and pain…aha…the association with discomfort! The horse did not know the cause of his pain, but would understandably associate the act of being ridden or driven to cause pain. I was the stupid one here; I had failed to think like the horse.

My best ally in training a horse was one of my experienced horses. I saddled up Aleser, the happy go lucky one, or Charlie, the sensitive one, or Spinnaker, the don't mess around with me mare, or Major, the challenging one, and took Lucky out for a "ride." I was not on his back, yet above him and able to control him from my mount. He had little choice but to follow along and take the commands, not just from me, but also from my horse.

We covered a lot of miles. Lucky learned the cue for trot, how to hold back going down hill and how to dodge trees along the trail. His mentors were unforgiving. Should he not want to keep up or turn, the sheer force of having another horse move him was a lesson enough. My horses maintained the herd concept, join up or get out. I eventually worked up to placing a bit in his mouth, and then a saddle on his back as we trotted and cantered the Vermont hills. Lucky figured out, in an exceptionally quick amount of time, that the work did not hurt; the pain was not coming back.

Yet, there remained a resistance. It was subtle; a stomp of a foot, hesitation before connecting to a command or reluctance in his gait. There was still something not fluid in Lucky's performance even though I was able to ride him. Seven months had passed, and despite the impressive change in this horse, I knew the journey was not complete. His owner understood; I could take the time to make him whole.

Horses are funny creatures. A huge truck coming at them on a roadway can cause less concern than a blowing leaf. Horses who would boldly jump over four-foot fences might balk at crossing over a fallen tree. I knew that Lucky's nemesis was water. He simply did not like it. He did his best to avoid puddles and had, since a colt, argued at water crossings. It was an area in our training sessions where Lucky blocked me out; it was that important. It was the battle that would win the war; the question was, how to do it?

As the spring melt opened up my pastures, it offered the opportunity to use the stream that led to one of the fields as Lucky's training ground. By this point, he was happily living in my herd, quite the regular fellow and very comfortable in that setting. My horses knew, the moment I opened the gate, that luscious spring grass lay beyond and so, kicking up their heels, they tore down the path and across the stream. All but Lucky.

Toes at water's edge, Lucky stopped dead. Water, no, no, not water. Lucky, even with the disappearance of his herd, answered to his instinct of not trusting water. He whinnied, and they whinnied back, but no pleading by him would cause them to leave the luscious, new grass. Lucky remained alone on his side of the stream. The stage was set for Lucky to make the decision that would change him…or not.

For a horse not to follow his herd is against thousands of years of survival instinct. The herd was safety. Yet Lucky stood at the bank of that stream for two days. The herd would cross back to come to the barn to see if I was going to toss out some hay for them, and Lucky would rejoice. It was short lived, as the newly emerging grass, across the stream, was all I was willing to offer. We could hear Lucky's pitiful whinnies from the house, but he still would not cross.

My neighbors have a gelding who will not cross their stream. He does not care if the other horses leave or that he spends the day eating meager weeds while they chomp on long grass. Whatever his horse sense says, nothing over-powers his distaste for that water. I knew a foal who refused to follow his mother through a tiny little stream and would wait on his side until she returned, regardless of her entreaties. Perhaps Lucky would be like them?

The husband, somewhat disturbed by my cavalier attitude about Lucky's "suffering," dragged several bales of hay down to and across the steam to help entice him to cross. It did not work.

"Do not, and I really mean this, do not try to get him across," I said sternly.

"But."

"Do not," I repeated, seeing the pain he was feeling for the horse. "He has to work this out on his own. If you or I were to spend what could be hours getting him to cross, he would only resent us more. He still thinks that he is being "made" to do things, anything, including crossing water. He has to overcome this in order to understand that he can overcome everything else."

"But…"

"He will do it, give him the chance."

What I did not know at that time was that his owner was in

California doing research, but her mind kept coming back to Lucky. Using sand play often helped her clarify the issues blocking her from writing. She had many objects to add to the sand, from human characters, to leaves and rocks. As she sculpted the sand with her hands, she placed a small, dark horse into the sand. Then she placed a plastic centipede which, when turned on its side, became a barrier. Without thinking why, she sunk it in the sand and straddled the horse over it.

On the third day, he crossed.

That evening his owner called. "Did something happen with Lucky recently?" she asked.

"As a matter of fact, it did," and I told her about crossing the stream.

Not only did Lucky cross the steam, he never hesitated again. He ran with the herd, flying across, as if he had done it every day of his life. And in his training, the stomping stopped. The hesitation was gone. He grasped my cues and encouragements with a new sense of confidence and trust. He had, indeed, crossed the stream to the other side.

The day before he was to return home, I stood with Lucky in the pasture. He came to me, as was now his habit, and stood inches from my face in a manner that caused us to share the same air. It was a gesture of intimacy, being so close yet not touching. It showed trust and respect and was, indeed, a great compliment. I stroked his lovely neck, now relaxed and beautiful, hardly the way in which it had come to me. I could feel his breath, soft and trustful, hardly the way it had come to me. I could not even remember where I had left the whip that I never was without when he had come to me. We stood together for a long time, that last time, and I knew that part of his soul and mine, would always travel together. He was, indeed, lucky.

A stubborn horse walks behind you,
An impatient horse walks in front of you,
But a noble companion walks beside you

TOTEM

My horse, trotting along a wooded trail, jumped a bit forward, not bad, but enough for me to look back to see if perhaps a branch had attached itself to his tail. Nothing. He jumped again. This time I stopped, the horse stepped to the side of the trail, and a forty pound pig trotted on past. The pig belonged to my neighbor, Steve, and was wont to roam the woods on his own. Neither the pig, nor my horse, seemed bothered by the encounter.

The pig had somehow managed to hitch a ride in one of Steve's horse trailers when he was transporting animals from his winter home in Georgia to the summer one in Vermont. He was a rather handsome Vietnamese pot-bellied pig, but not truly tame enough to call a pet. He was as black as night with thick bristles standing straight up on his head and back which gave him the appearance of a large porcupine. He free-roamed the farm, cruising from pasture to pasture to snarffle up feed dropped by the horses when they were fed. The pig had incredible timing and had gained more than a few pounds since he had arrived in Vermont.

Since horses meant food to him, he liked horses. He would often trot along behind a horse or group of horses when they were ridden on the farm's trails. As the horses got used to him, the pig got bolder. A slight poke with his snout would make the horse jump a bit forward giving the pig room to pass at a trot and onto his business.

The pig soon discovered a neighbor's barn. He showed up one morning at feeding time and stood in the aisle making pig noises. The neighbor, alarmed and confused, threw some feed at him and ran. The pig came back the next morning. The neighbor, frantic, called the local constable who called Steve and the pig was retrieved. The next morning, the pig was back. This time the neighbor called Steve directly but he was not home.

"At first I thought it was a huge porcupine," said Linda, "then I realized it was just a porker." "It's just easier to feed him than try to shoo him out of the barn. He just comes right back. I've actually gotten to like the little guy." The pig showed up in her barn every morning after that.

We had all become accustomed to the pig by midsummer. Periodically, Steve would get a call from the constable saying that the pig had been sighted heading towards Reading, the next town, and he could not be responsible for the pig's well being once he left his jurisdiction. Rumor had it that the Reading folk ate pigs.

The only reason the pig enjoyed such freedom and tolerance was because no one could catch him. His football shaped body defied a handhold and his months of wandering had him in wicked good shape to run. Pigs are fast! Steve did have a fifty-dollar reward for anyone who could pen him up, but no one had yet succeeded.

In mid-July, Steve's farm became the home of the Vermont One-Hundred Mile Ride and Run, an event that put both horses and runners across one hundred miles of trail in one day. For humans, the sport is called "ultra-marathoning." Runners from all over the world, three hundred of them, camped at the farm and at four o'clock in the morning started the race. This is an extreme sport and attracts some compulsive personality types.

Running one-hundred miles is not exactly everyone's idea of sport. Personally, it has never crossed my mind. But, as the event demonstrates every year, there are a lot of athletes out there that think that running one-hundred miles in twenty-four hours is the ultimate experience. This was demonstrated by the many letters that we, the organizers, receive after the race. The letters tell of the magical experience of running through the night reaching an internal rhythm with the plants and animals in the woods, and visions that direct their lives. It is probably the dehydration and sleep deprivation talking, but they cling to their stories.

One particular story stood out. This runner was trying for the third time to reach the finish line within the twenty-four hour limit. He had trained hard and mapped out a time line so he could finally accomplish his goal. The runners are allowed to pick up a pace runner at sixty miles. The pace runner is given instruction beforehand as to how the runner wants to complete the next forty miles. Some runners just want company and support, others, like this man, wanted to be kept on a time line, no matter what.

The story starts out with his running into the dawn, crossing the Ottauquechee River and climbing over the Appalachian Trail. All beautiful, all going as planned. The runner went into some detail about having a cramp at thirty-six miles but being able to run out of it and keep to his time-line. At sixty miles, he connected with his pace runner and both decided that if he were to attain his goal, there could be no pauses, no extra time to smell the roses; just running. By midnight, he was on the last four-mile stretch of hilly trail that crossed onto Steve's farm for the finish. More than once he told his pacer not to allow him to stop, not for anything.

A full moon had broken through the clouds and the woods took on fairy-like appearance in the silver light. The runner was exhausted but determined. The story dwells on the surreal trees and how each step felt as he was climbing a mountain. He became aware of time slowing down, and no matter how hard he tried, he could not move forward. Suddenly standing before him in a shard of moonlight, stood the biggest porcupine he had ever seen. The porcupine stopped and met his gaze, absorbing his soul and gifting him the strength to finish his quest. The animal was gone as quickly as it had appeared. Convinced that he had just seen his totem animal, the porcupine, the runner stopped for a second to take this all in before his pacer nudged him on.

The pacer had not seen the porcupine, giving the runner all the more reason to believe that the vision was for him and him only. He finished within his goal, accepting his medal with beaming pride. Even better, he now knew that the porcupine would be his guide through life and he was planning on having a small tattoo of the animal placed on his ankle. The story finished thanking us for allowing him to have such a life changing experience.

I called Steve and read him the story.

"Hmm", he said.

"Any idea where your pig was that night?" I asked.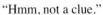

"Hmm, not a clue."

Neither of us had the heart to inform the runner that his totem animal was unquestionably a pot-bellied pig.

FEEDING CATS

Spend some time in the pet aisle of any grocery store and you will find pet owners staring blankly at the cornucopia of pet foods offered. The dog owners grab a bag of dry food and throw in a six-pack of canned food, and move on. But the cat owners dwell. Not wanting to return home with the "wrong" food, yet again, they have copious notes on their grocery list citing the types of cat food that are NOT acceptable to their feline house partners. You can see the distress on their faces, the hesitation as they reach for a can. "Is this the one Fluffy liked, or was it the can with the pretty white cat? No, Fluffy only ate that once. Perhaps the variety pack would have something Fluffy likes; at least there is one chance out of ten choices. Then, maybe not."

One has to wonder if the cat food industry is driven by a group of neurotic cat owners who feel the pressure continually to expand the variety of choices as dictated by their own cats? No matter what the food product, it can be had grilled, sliced, marinated, minced, roasted, chunky, flaked or with gravy. It appears to be just a matter of time before every house cat figures this out and snubs yet another form of cat food, knowing full well that something new is on the horizon.

As each flavor is passed up: fine cuts with chicken and gravy, prime filets of beef with gravy, ocean whitefish and tuna with sauce, another emerges: classic pate beef and chicken entrée, meaty bits with lamb and rice in gravy, grilled tuna feast in gravy, marinated morsels of turkey, thus creating an almost infinite variety of product. As the cat food gets more specialized, the names become more like something you would see as an entrée at a five-star restaurant: New England crab cakes, sesame chicken, yellow fin tuna, seafood and tomato bisque. With flavors like that, why aren't we eating cat food?

Our cats were unquestionably in tune with the cat food industry. Every new can that was opened and presented to the cats had great expectations; Strubble Peter twirled in circles in excitement; Gypsy Rose Lee tried to paw the can from my hands; Bob meowed quietly; and Miss Marple sat politely by her dish waiting to be served. Amelia Ear-heart (as dictated by her distinct coloration) was the most honest of the bunch, willing to give everything a try before leaving the rest uneaten.

I would expound on the fine qualities of the cat food by reading the label to them, "seafood dinner - whitefish, salmon and tuna blended into a delicious pate. Doesn't that sound nice?" Strubble Peter would dive into the first spoonful and suddenly realize that he was not crazy about seafood this week as he was last week. Gypsy inhaled her portion before I got the next one to Bob. He sniffs it, meows, and then sits down to decide whether or not it is edible. He better be quick, or Gypsy or Amelia was going to eat it for him. Miss Marple, always with the best of manners, refuses to offer an opinion until the food has warmed on the plate, and, even then, shows the correct amount of restraint before acknowledging that, in fact, dinner has been served.

The success of each feeding would inversely diminish with the next serving after the cat food had spent time in the refrigerator, ick; it is now cold, hard, less tasty, perhaps even inedible. The cat food industry knows that only too well as indicated by the increasingly smaller and smaller size cans offered at ridiculously high prices. One could feed a horse on what all of those cat food cans would cost in a year!

I had to be sharp and pay attention to what food was served previously in order to keep the cats interested in the next opened can. "Chicken and giblets," I'd say, "that sounds yummy."

When you stop to think about it, the cat food can has nothing to do with what a cat would be able to catch and eat for itself. Ever see a cat out crabbing? Fishing for yellow fin tuna? Running down a full size turkey? Grilling slices of beef? Cats, at least my cats, have happily eaten crickets, cluster flies, voles, mice, and an assortment of unfortunate birds. However, the shelf appeal of a can of chopped vole with bones and entrails in sauce probably would not sell.

Feeding cats was enough of a challenge without also having to medicate them. Miss Marple was the most vicious of cats when it came to pills despite her demure appearance. I would rather shove my hand down the garbage disposal than pop a pill down her throat. Instead, I tried a liquid form of her thyroid medication that I ordered at my pharmacy. Miss Marple had her own account. I would send the husband into town, and he would walk up to the nice lady at the counter and ask, "Miss Marple's medication please."

"Do you have a form of ID, sir?"

"Will a picture of the cat do?"

"Are you authorized to sign for this, sir?"

"I am sure I am, although the cat has never actually said so."

"Here you go, I just love Agatha Christy mysteries; please give Miss Marple my regards."

The medication was cloaked in fish oil, the pharmacist's attempt to outsmart a cat who could detect medication a mile off. The assumption was that any cat worth her whiskers would love fish oil. The fish oil was contained in a plastic bottle with a childproof lid and sealed in a plastic bag. It was a pretty reasonable bet that a child would rather endure a trip to the dentist than try to open a bottle, no matter how tightly sealed, which exuded the odor of a breeding colony of sea lions.

The odor was none too pleasant to have in the house, although it announced to the cats, no matter where they were on our one hundred and twenty acre farm, it was feeding time. The molecular weight of that odor was so heavy that when it entered a human's olfactory canal it lay there for hours. Any cat food, when dressed with the oil, took on the all the characteristics of that breeding colony of sea lions. This occurred twice a day for over a year. I was ecstatic when Miss Marple finally decided to turn it down. The prospect of returning to putting a pill down her throat truly looked good.

One attempt to pill her was all it took to for me again to find a way of getting her to eat the pill in food. My arm was healing nicely when I came up with the idea of slicing a slit into a hunk of raw chicken and stuffing the pill inside, kind of like a pita pocket. Miss Marple ate the chicken but more often than not the pill would be spat out, sometimes sticking to the fur of another cat. I had to be quick enough to retrieve the pill for fear that all of my cats would end up with thyroid problems. I tried making meatballs with cat food. Freshly opened cat can contents were slimy and unwieldy for making meatballs, the pill often left at the bottom of the dish. Refrigerated can contents were more pliable, but better than half of the time, left by the cat; after all, it was old and cold.

The search went on for cat food with the right texture to roll into a meatball fresh from the can. Not only did we read the label for hints of texture, we peered at the tiny picture of the cat food on the can. Flaked, bits, or chunks were out. We needed ground up, homogenized, old-lady cat food that could be swallowed, not necessarily chewed. Somewhere during this tedious process, I accidentally bought dog food.

Can you believe it, the solution was canned dog food? Freshly opened the texture was perfect to roll up a pill into a meatball. One or two licks and the thing stuck to the cat's tongue, and she had little choice but to swallow it, pill and all. Success! Amazingly, the other cats thought the dog food pretty decent fare as well; whether that was because it was so new and different, or because they sensed the revenge of eating "their" food. Eventually, the smell of the breeding colony of sea lions faded from the house, Miss Marple prospered, and the feeding of cats became a simple and civilized event. The next time you need a little entertainment visit the cat food aisle. There will always be someone there desperately trying to find something their cats will like. Don't suggest dog food, it will spoil the cat's fun.

"I gave an order to a cat, and the cat gave it to its tail"
- Chinese Proverb

The following four articles appeared in <u>The Chronicle of the Horse,</u> a national publication of renowned status when it came to covering the sport of fox hunting. I sent the articles to them to see if they had a sense of humor, which indeed they did, and the following is what they printed four seasons straight.

—ᴜᴜ—

THE "GRUNDSOW HUNT" of LEHIGH COUNTY

Lehigh County, Pa. has never had a hunt, until now. Located in the heart of Pennsylvania Dutch country, Thorny Hills Farms decided it was about time to organize their small group of adventurous riders into a hunt. The big question was; are there any fox? No, but plenty of ground hogs, "grundsows" to the locals, well known as a crafty and fierce adversary for farm dogs. The farm dogs consisted of a dachshund puppy, an ancient golden retriever long retired, and a very willing German Shepherd named Waabb. Waabb became the "pack of hounds" and during "cubbing" sent many a ground hog to heaven. According to whipper-in, Sue Greenall, the one advantage of hunting with German Shepherds is that property owners don't give you much trouble.

November 19, marked the opening of the hunt with riders coming as far away as England. Because of the unique nature of the hunt, the field was very carefully selected, as the groundhog is quite difficult to hunt. "This is strictly an invitational hunt and I was honored to be invited," remarked Betsey Nicoll of Ambler, Pa. Opening the ceremony was Bob Walter who used a flow chart to explain the differences between a ground hog and wart hogs, road hogs, and being a hog. Reverend Edwards blessed the hound, a stirrup cup of apple-jack was downed and the hunt was off over twelve miles of rolling farmland pocked with groundhog holes. Despite the fleetness of the horses, the cunning of the hound and the skill of the riders, not a groundhog was sighted, but a grand time was had by all. Over the hunt breakfast of waffles and champagne, someone discovered that groundhogs go into hibernation for the winter. When master of the hunt, John Greenall, was asked about this, he remarked, "who needs a groundhog to have fun, anyway. As long as we know they're out there, we'll be hunting."

SECOND ANNUAL "GRUNDSOW" HUNT
OF LEHIGH COUNTY, PA.

It was with great anticipation that rider's looked to see if they had been invited to the second annual "grundsow" hunt of Lehigh County. Being a private hunt, and being only once a year, getting an invitation meant that you were considered a) a good rider b) a good sport and c) a good time. The third quality seemed to be the determining factor as not all of the participants turned out to be good riders or good sports, but they all had a good time.

Started last season, by John and Sue Greenall, because it was discovered that not only didn't Lehigh County have a hunt, it had NEVER had a hunt. Aghast at this, the Greenall's put together an outstanding pack of German Shepherds and scoured the countryside for their prey, the groundhog, "grundsow" to the locals. Despite the quality of the field, ne'er a groundhog was sighted until spring.

This November 18, the field had nearly doubled in size, with riders coming from as far away as Germany. Silke Stiefel had heard about the hunt from last year's rider, Betsy Nicoll, of Ambler, Pa., and planned her tour of the U.S. to include the hunt. "We don't have such things at home", she commented, "nor do we have groundhogs. Just hedgehogs." Two other new riders, Dr. Greg Lang and Mitchell Masters, were Lehigh County residents who had learned to ride just to be included on the hunt. Unfortunately, when one of the riders was kicked in the leg, it turned out that Dr. Lang was an Obstetrician, commenting, "areas below the knee are grey areas to me."

The sudden weather changed from Indian summer to almost winter, put the horses in a ready mood for the chase. The traditional blessing of the Shepherds was again done by Rev. Edwards, and a toast of applejack to good riding by master John Greenall. The hunt covered over 18 miles of mostly new trails this year and for a short time, the field thought it had a run on a groundhog, but it turned out to be the farmer's cat. Master Greenall was forced to call a foul and the chase was ended. However, the riders all looked forward to the hunt's only jump, a brush affair set up in the woods.

Unfortunately, the second horse over, Cindy Milnazik's Percheron mare, Daisy, rendered the jump into nothing but twigs. It was unanimously decided that all Percherons jump last next year.

Since the weather was so brisk, a brandy stop was set up at the farm of Patrick Crowley, which is the reason why he was invited on the hunt. It took some prodding to get some of the riders back on their horses, and it became evident why when one parted from her horse, giggling through her hiccups, on the first hill. A sudden snow squall surrounded the riders for their last four miles, blinding those with glasses and turning pink unmuffed ears.

The hunt breakfast of hot cider and sandwiches was followed by a plunge in the hot tub. "Running through those snowflakes to the tub was the hardest part of the ride," said Bob Walter. This year's hunt was so full of fun and excitement that no one seemed to notice the lack of groundhogs.

—᙮—

THE GRUNDSOWERS RIDE AGAIN

On the second day of the second month, a small furry brown creature emerges from his hole to decide the fate of our winter. But few people realize that he is also the polestar of the Thorny Hills Farm Annual Grundsow Hunt, held in its third year on December 3, in rural Lehigh County, Pa. Having been ballyhooed by word of mouth, and this publication, John, Greenall, master, was inundated by requests for invitations this year. "We must be very selective," explained Greenall, "for only the fleetest and most stalwart hunting horses need be brought, as the groundhog is a cunning and worthy adversary."

"The thought of a hunt which chased groundhogs with German Shepherds spurred me to solicit an invitation," tells Davida Waters, of Pickering Hunt Country. "When I was told that anyone who brought their own Shepherd to add to the pack got to ride as a whipper-in, I couldn't wait." Upon receiving her invitation, Davida devoted most of her time conditioning her Shepherd alongside her AERC National Champion Endurance Horse, "Cloud Valley." He arrived in fine shape. Another newcomer was Bill Vandetta, well known as the ringmaster at Devon and the Washington International Shows. Bill's addition to the hunt was sounding the horn, which stimulated the nervous systems of some of the horses unaccustomed to such finery.

The weather was promising when riders gathered at the barn for the blessing of the "hounds" and the traditional stirrup cup of applejack. Seasoned grundsower, Lynn Braddick, of Collegeville, Pa., was flagged from the cup due to her excessive giggling last season. Four riders were presented with colors, a pink sweatshirt with a ground hog "fur" collar. Master John Greenall, whipper-in Sue Greenall, Bob Walter and Betsey Nicol wore their new finery with pride. Lynn was heard to say, "If I don't giggle so much this year, maybe I'll get my colors." We'll see, Lynn.

A new addition was made to the hunt this year, jumps. "Since we have never sighted any groundhogs, we decided to add excitement by building some jumps. We don't care if anyone goes over them or not, but they look good in the video," explained course designer, Bob Walter, of Warrington, Pa. The first half of the hunt proved to be a fast pace. "We had brunch reservations, so we had to make up the time after a late start," explained Master Greenall. 'That, and Dr. Lang had to deliver a baby at one." The mid-point refreshment stop, held at squire Crowley's farm offered a spread of delicious goodies and grundsow grog. For those unaccustomed to such a luxury at other hunts, it was a welcome surprise.

The second half of the hunt took the riders through new territory. While galloping across a wondrously open cornfield, a fox was sighted. "Talk about being at the wrong place at the wrong time," exclaimed Mitchell Masters, as he reluctantly turned his horse to follow the Shepherds that were exploring yet another groundhog hole. "If this were summer, we'd be stepping all over those groundhogs, but, alas, such is the nature of this hunt," explained the Greenalls.

The horses were put up while the stalwart grundsowers enjoyed a hearty brunch at a nearby restaurant. Mr. Vandetta was heard querying Mr. Greenall, "Do you always ride like this?" "Only once a year," was his reply, "the rest of the time we're in training."

—w—

THE GRUNDSOW HUNT OF LEHIGH COUNTY, PA.

For the past four years, Lehigh County, Pa., has distinguished itself by having one, and only one, hunt. But as the locals would say, "Such a hunt!" Upon discovering that there were no local hunts, John and Sue Greenall turned their Thorny Hills Farm into a one-day hunting box, this year the occasion being November 24, 1991. Not only did the field double this year, it tripled with nineteen "fleet and most stalwart hunting horses, as the groundhog, AKA grundsow, is a cunning and worthy adversary."

Held in the heart of the rolling hills of Pennsylvania Dutch country, just loaded with hex signs, covered bridges, and groundhogs, the hunt takes on a local flavor. Hence, the use of German Shepherds to track the quarry does not seem to turn any heads. Everyone dresses as they like and colors are a fur trimmed hot pink sweatshirt. Earning colors this year were Lynn Braddick, of Collegeville, Pa., as after four years, she finally managed to stay with her horse for the complete hunt, and

Dr. Greg Lang, of Orefield, Pa., whose beeper finally failed to beep so he got to complete a hunt. Lynn was especially thrilled with her sweatshirt as "pink is my color."

Having stood at the sidelines in the past, three junior riders managed to convince master John Greenall to allow them to ride the first half of the hunt. Mounted on fire-breathing ponies, they negotiated the course in good form, with only a few "close ones". In fact, it was the geriatric pony, So-Fat, that realized that she knew a short cut to barn, giving Dr. Lang's daughter, Jessie, quite a ride until Bob Walter demonstrated the swiftness and adroitness of his Percheron/TB cross and cut them off at the pass. "All that dressage training really paid off," was Bob's comment.

Riding as an honorary whipper in, because she brought her own Shepherd, was Melanie McCarthy a regular with the Pickering Hunt. Not only did this Shepherd stay up with the famous "Greenall grundsowers", but also earned the admiration of all as she has only three legs! "I adopted her that way from the local pound, and she's surely proven herself today," beamed Melanie.

This year there was a great deal of jumping, as the course wound its way over the newly built cross-country course at Thorny Hills. "One is somewhat limited to what can be built when the majority our boarders are on small ponies," explained course designer Sue Greenall. "I sneak an extra log in every so often, but the kids are getting wise to me." All the same, everyone had a good go over the course, continuing on for a six mile loop that brought them back to the traditional mid-point stop at squire Crowley's.

When Lady Crowley fell off the porch and broke her leg three days before the hunt, a mad search was made to find a new hostess. Pressed into service was local landowner, Connie Galligher, whose exposure to equines was through Quarter Horses. Exhausted after passing out

hot cider, shortbread cookies and "meadow muffins" to the ravenous riders, and Shepherds, she was rather happy to see the hunt set off for the second half of the ride. She was overheard saying, "If they wore Western hats, we could call it "The Grundsow Round-up!"

The horses were put up while the stalwart riders enjoyed a hearty brunch at a nearby restaurant. A toast was made to the skill and cunningness of the groundhog, who once again, eluded both Shepherds and huntsman. "Have they ever sighted a groundhog?" one of the new riders was heard to ask. "Once," explained master Greenall, "but it turnout out to only be his shadow."

RAIN COATS

The patter of rain on my window did not offer pleasant thoughts even as I slept. It had been raining all night; come to think of it, it had been raining all week. Before I went to bed I had checked with the weatherman, who was notorious for being off the mark sixty percent of the time, and he promised intermittent showers all night, heavy rain in the morning tapering off to light rain in the afternoon. I just loved the creative ways the weatherman had to describe a rainy day and, it would figure, that this would be the one time he was right.

I was working on any valid excuse I could come up with to bow out of riding without having my friends call me a wimp. Nothing short of a broken leg would fly as an excuse, and the odds of breaking my leg while still in bed were slim.

It is not like I hadn't ridden in the rain before. Heck, I had ridden one-hundred mile endurance rides in the rain; start to finish. That is why I knew that I hated getting wet. I was no fan of having my boots fill with water and listening to the slosh-slosh every time I put weight into the stirrup, which was every time the horse took a step. Finding one's feet all wrinkly with the pallor of a codfish was icky. Wearing wet riding tights for more than a few hours resulted in nasty little bite-sized marks on the inside of one's legs from the folds those pants could not help make when wet. Worse would be if the riding tights got wet, dried, got wet, dried, over and over. They tightened like a gorilla grip around one's leg, leaving more bite-sized marks. Sports bras were no more kind.

Buoyed by the claims of sales personnel who maintain that their product will keep one dry while riding, I rode continually into disappointment. First, rain finds its way up the sleeve of every raincoat made until one slaps a rubber band around the wrist. Second, at some point, usually right after you have congratulated yourself on what a spiffing raincoat you have, a tiny drip of water trickles down your back. It is just one drip. But it has company. Lots of company. Did the manufacturer take into account that while wearing a riding helmet the rain is funneled directly down your neck? Without a neckerchief tied snugly around your collar, every raincoat will promise that little pleasure.

No raincoat had ever been made to keep me dry on a horse. Those fancy fiber coats that claim to be waterproof? Three hours of driving rain later there is a slight dampness to the coat that develops into a heavy spot on your back until you realize that the coat is sticking to you because, imagine that, it is wet. Waxed coats? Imagine a full day of riding in a coat that slowly, ever so slowly, wicks up enough water to make the coat weigh the equivalent of a gorilla on your back. Good luck getting off the horse and managing to stand up straight wearing one of those.

One time, my friend Dinah, talked me into riding in a garbage bag. "See," she said, "I cut a head hole and two arm holes and put slits up front and back, so we will fit right over the horse and be snug and dry right down to our feet."

The garbage bags were the size of body bags, hanging down to the ground when we walked. Had she not cut the slits up the middle we would have toppled right over on the first step. Still, I was willing to give it a try, how bad could it be?

The first challenge was getting them on. It had not started to rain until half way through the ride. Seasoned veterans as our horses were, they had never seen a billowing black garbage bag flap about behind their heads when we tried to put them on while still mounted. The horses took a vote and decided, en masse, to bolt and run. Running into the wind and rain only produced more billowing and flapping much to the dismay of our astonished mounts. Only good manners re- sulted in their finally stopping, not daring to move, until we got things under control.

Dismounted, and with calculated care, we slid on the garbage bags. As quietly as we could we remounted, all the while speaking reas- suring words to our horses, and continued down the trail. The rain increased, and the bags did keep out the water. Things went well for a while; until the wind picked up. Gusts of air would find their way under the bag and inflate us into puffy black clouds. While puffed, the rain would blow in with the effect of being in an upside down shower. The puffed bags would deflate, flap, and inflate at unpredictable repeti- tions. This action played with the nervous systems of the horses who were still getting over the first experience.

Caught out in the wind over open trail for some time, we had no other option but to ride using one hand trying to hold down the gar- bage bag with the other hand in control the horse. The horses were gaining speed with each puff we failed to control. We soared along, unable to say much to each other over the sound of the flapping bags. I would have liked to say, "some bright idea this was," but I knew my friend was thinking the same.

At last, in the shelter of trees in a wood, we were able to stop and

consider our options. Removing the bags would have seemed logical, but it meant that we would be drenched for the remainder of the ride. Futile attempts to tear the plastic to shorten the bags proved that one could ship a wildcat inside one with not a care. We ended up stuffing the long part of the bag into our boots, which produced less puffing but a whole lot more flapping noise when we finally returned to the trail. We were practically deaf, as were our horses, by the end of the day.

Hundreds of dollars and countless raincoats later, I have finally settled on a six-dollar plastic raincoat. They are not perfect, but much less disappointing for the price. I have a most unbecoming helmet cover that makes me look like a cone head but it keeps the water from dripping down my neck. I have also discovered that baggies, the ones you get at the store kind of baggie, kept my feet dry longer than any special kind of sock. I am no fashion statement, but I know how to dress to ride in rainy weather.

I rode that day in the rain; why not?

There are only two emotions that belong in the saddle;
One is a sense of humor
The other is patience.

Houdini

For fifteen dollars, hard earned money when one is thirteen, I purchased my first pony. When I first laid eyes on Pepper, I thought he was a Standard Poodle! Standing only thirty-seven inches high, his boxy little body grew a winter coat that would embarrass a sheep. Pepper never failed to offer a nicker and a gentle nuzzle whenever he saw me.

I tried to ride him, but my feet dragged the ground. Plus, he knew a few tricks that would put a rider on the ground faster than one could say, "bad pony." I decided to drive him, and lacking a harness or cart, I made a harness out of rope and hooked him to a toboggan. I was thirteen; I did not know any better. Pepper was an exceptionally good sport about it and, once I got the bugs worked out, we had a blast. I did need a sturdy pair of boots for brakes.

Over the next fifteen years, Pepper entertained many of my friends and their children. He was hugely popular at birthday parties and family picnics. One birthday party was well on its way when it started to rain, so they brought him into the house. There the children rode him around the living room while playing Pin the Tail on the Donkey. Once, he was returned to me in the backseat of a convertible. He easily earned a truly special spot in everyone's heart.

Pepper's one annoying habit was his ability to escape any form of fencing I challenged him with. It was a life long competition. The escapes were followed by forays around the neighborhood where he left a trail of divots on manicured lawns. I spent a goodly deal of my

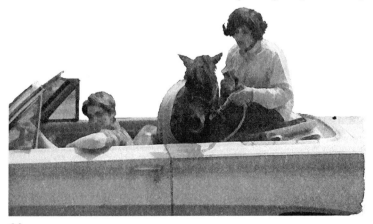

youth tamping down those divots and apologizing for my little friend. Houdini was no match for this pony.

I was teaching school and on my own farm when Pepper reached his mid-twenties. Winter had us in full grip and doing barn chores was a bear of a job. Everything was frozen and everything took more time and effort than usual. I do remember seeing Pepper standing with his hind leg cocked, but he was out of mind when I had to deal with a frozen water trough. Some time later, I again noticed Pepper standing, in the same spot, with his hind leg cocked. Horses do not stand perfectly still for that long. As I approached him, I looked at his hind leg thinking perhaps he was caught in something. When I reached to move the leg, the sensation I experienced sent shivers straight down my spine. The leg moved, but in pieces, like beads on a string. He had broken, no shattered, his left hind leg!

It was a full minute before I could collect myself. "They shoot horses, don't they" brought the horrible reality of the situation to surface. Through my tears, I cradled his head to tell him his fate. My pony looked back at me with his big round eyes and told me that he expected me to help him. In a situation like this; it would require a miracle. I never hesitated; I would do whatever it took.

My veterinarian never suggested the obvious alternative. Instead, he helped me contact the University of Pennsylvania New Bolton Veterinary Clinic where we would get the singular care the situation called for. He secured a pillow around the broken leg and shoved hay bales under Pepper, so he could brace himself in the horse trailer. Friends arrived to drive the truck while I rode in the trailer for a cold, grueling three hour trip to the clinic.

Dr. Midge Leach headed up the extremely competent staff that treated Pepper. The hours of X-rays, examinations, and consultations began. Pepper was a true equine geriatric and not too many people bring old ponies with broken legs into the New Bolton clinic. I believe I still hold that record. Despite his condition, Pepper managed to charm the staff off their feet. Because of his shaggy winter coat, they nicknamed him "Baby Bison" and fell in love with him on the spot. Who could help not to? They put the nicest fiberglass cast on his leg and added a spoonful of love and a pound of luck. After five days at the clinic, they sent Pepper home to heal.

The next six months saw Pepper adjusting extremely, no, exceptionally well to his cast. He shifted his weight a little to the right, adjusted his stride, and could move right along "cloppity, cloppity, thud" wearing that cast. As far as he was concerned, life returned to normal. He still wiggled through my fences and ran around the yard, albeit a tad slower, to find tender nibbles of grass. Even with the cast on, he could out run me. He never lost his optimism and joy of life.

I dreaded the removal of that cast, for if the leg had not completely healed; it was all over. One last trip to New Bolton where the entire staff who had treated Pepper showed up for the crucial moment. The shriveled leg looked hardly sturdy enough to hold him, but Pepper tested it, took a step, and walked off as if he knew all along that he would be fine. We all let out a long sigh of relief.

His x-rays still remain at New Bolton as being one of the most catastrophic bone fractures they ever dealt with. And I do believe, at age twenty-seven, he was the oldest equine to have survived such an ordeal. Pepper lived five more happy years and showed just a hint of a limp for his experience. His legendary escapes from my fences never ceased; and he would barrel over a lawn at a full gallop any time he wanted to leave some divots for me to tamp down.

THE SNEEZE

Being allergic to just about everything on planet Earth, I am accustomed to walking around with wads of tissue in my pockets and a runny nose. I sniffle and sneeze on a regular basis, especially when in the barn where I am exposed to hay, dust, cat hair, horsehair and whatever blows through the doors. The husband, on the other hand, rarely sneezes. But when he does, his sneezes are like putting a little money into an investment portfolio where it grows and grows into something substantial when it comes out. When he sneezes, he scares the cats and makes the dogs bark.

This is especially hard on Bob. Bob is a Manx cat whom we took home from our good friends' barn in Pennsylvania. They are always so clever to "just happen to have" a kitten whenever we visit. Who can pass up a kitten? Bob, if a person, would be a recluse who only came out of his cave on perfect sunny days when no one was around. Our house sitter, after three years, did not even know we had a fourth cat.

"Where does he live?"

"In the basement,' I said, "He's kind of shy."

His favorite spot was in a big beanbag chair my cousin left here ten years ago. She will not let me throw it out because she is sure they will come back in style. If it does, there will be ten years of Bob hair to get through before she finds the chair again!

Bob sneaks up from the safety of the basement whenever he senses I am alone in the house. One on one, Bob is a terrific cat. He will reach for me to pick him up, roll over to have his belly rubbed and cuddle up on the couch. The husband is barely tolerated and has perhaps touched Bob twice, both times an error of judgment by Bob. This bothers the husband to no end as he is a true animal lover, but if it were not for that sneeze, things might have been different.

The built up power of the husband's sneeze has the ability to lift Bob straight off the floor. Should he be cuddling with me on the couch, his claws dig into my leg like Apollo Ono's skates at the start of a short track race. He can make the door to the basement in Olympic time and won't be seen for days, perhaps weeks.

"Poor Bob," I mutter, rubbing the claw digs out of my leg.

"Must you sneeze like that?"

"I have sneezed this way all of my life," returns the husband, "one would think that cat would get used to it."

"No one," I pointed out, "gets used to it."

It is not as if there is any warning to the sneeze. I sniffle and make little noises, and then sneeze. Not the husband. All is quiet, birds are singing, the wind rustling through the trees, and "ACHOO!!!!" like a sonic boom, the sneeze deafens those in its way. It has truly gotten worse over the years.

The husband claims that his sneeze is just as much a surprise to him as it is to others. I beg to disagree; he at least knows it's coming.

I took the opportunity to point this out after finding that another of our animals took exception to the husband's sneeze. Our home raised colt and filly were going through their young horse training protocol which sometimes makes them a little nervous and unsure. I was riding along with the husband who was on a very judicious horse. My innocent mount was worrying about being attacked by a saber-toothed chipmunk or a horse eating rock, all things that a young horse's imagination conjure up. "ACHOO!!!" My unsuspecting horse spun one hundred eighty degrees to the left, wind ripping through my ears, and little snippets of my life flashing by. I felt as if I was riding Bob on one of his races for the basement! The colt landed with his legs splayed and tensed for another spin, should such the sound repeat itself. Picking some mane from my teeth, I raised myself up off his neck, glared at the husband and muttered, "I don't care what you do next, just do not sneeze!"

This incident sparked a number of discussions about sneezing etiquette. For the sake of those with fragile nervous systems, some form of warning should come before setting a sneeze loose. The husband did make an effort, but the sneeze continued to cause panic reactions of select animals in our care. Good judgment dictated that I not ride the colt in the presence of the husband and Bob continued to live in the basement. Then the husband went to Florida.

The husband travels a great deal in order to officiate at horse competitions as a judge. He gets to see a vast amount of the country and meets wonderful people. This trip to Florida was for a selection trial for four-in-hand driving horses vying for a spot on the United States Equestrian Federation Team and the upcoming World Equestrian Games in Kentucky. It was a pretty significant event.

In order to judge dressage, a prescribed set of movements one could liken to figure skating but done with a horse, booths are set up around the ring for the officials. One is at the far end of the ring and two are on the sides. The booth is just large enough for the judge and his scribe, and in cold weather, had plastic sides with only the front open. It was cold that year in Florida.

Driving a four-in-hand through a dressage test is no easy task. The driver, through his reins and voice, must give delicate and precise commands to the horses, sometimes having to divide the commands between the lead two and the back two. Years of training go into this level of performance, and the horses are selected for their obedience and ability to connect to their driver. It takes a huge amount of concentration on the part of the driver to communicate each subtle command to his horses throughout the test. Their attention is so sharply focused on the task that anything happening outside of their "bubble" is rarely noticed. I have often commented that a space ship could land next to the arena, and no one would notice until the test was over.

The four-in-hand in the ring was driven by America's top driver; he was a favorite for a team spot. The horses were alongside the husband's judging booth when it happened; "ACHOO!" The acoustic design of the plastic sides and open front magnified the sneeze by ten fold. Four thousand five hundred pounds of finely trained horseflesh leapt up off of the ground in unison, swinging their heads in clear dismay at a sound they had never encountered. The astonished driver, who had also jumped in his seat, adeptly regained control of his horses and continued with his test. But not without taking the opportunity to say "bless you" when he passed by the judge's booth next.

Bob wished he could have been there.

DASHING THROUGH THE SNOW

"Dashing through the snow - in a one horse open sleigh" was a way of life in Vermont for centuries and is still a popular type of recreation in the form of sleigh rallies. Perfect winter days are embellished by the sound of sleigh bells and the gliding of century old sleighs over the snow. We were no exception from those that brought out their horses whenever such an opportunity presented itself.

As lovely as sleigh rallies are, they come with their own set of challenges. At sub-zero temperatures, leather harness stiffens up, and gloved fingers have to struggle to fit it on the horse; the harness disappearing into the three inches of hair the horse is wearing at the time.

The husband and our friend, Ed, had harnessed up my pony for the Gentleman's Class in which Ed was driving. My pony, a seasoned veteran of years of driving competitions, was, in my mind, the best. As they entered the ring, I grabbed my camera for a shot that would become Ed's Christmas card. He looked just like a Currier & Ives century old print.

Cameras are about as happy with cold weather as leather harness, so I was keeping it as warm as possible under my coat between shots as the class progressed. Robin Groves, who would later compete at two World Driving Championships, was at my side offering commentary on the class.

"That bay Morgan is doing a nice job," she stated as the horses whirled past us.

"How is Ed doing, can you see him?"

"Here he comes; I think you can get a good shot, get your camera."

Rooting the camera from the depths of my winter coat, I focused in on Ed and my pony as they came into view.

"He looks good," said Robin, always willing to offer a compliment, "don't you think?"

Still busy with the camera focus, I was trying to figure out why the picture I saw through the viewfinder did not seem right. Ed, indeed, looked relaxed and happy, as did the pony. But something was wrong, very wrong, but I needed a better look, what was it...?

"Oh my!" I gasped, grabbing Robin by the arm. "We need to stop the class!"

"What?" she replied, completely unaware of the source of my panic.

"Just stop the class," I gasped, as I ran into the competition area waving frantically to Ed. Robin, her sharp eyes finding the cause of my panic, hurried behind me.

What we had seen was that the bit, the part of the bridle that controlled the pony, was not in her mouth but rather dangling under her chin, hidden by the long hairs of her chin. How Ed had managed to direct her was beyond me as most horses would have bolted or run. Not my pony, my best pony, for she simply accepted this error and performed perfectly.

As I said, the harness stiffens up and can disappear into the hair of the pony…and even experienced gloved fingers struggle to fit the harness on the horse and can make a mistake.

What a heroic pony.

Somewhere along the winter someone suggested skijoring - skiing behind a horse. Actually an age-old sport, reindeer were sometimes used as "horsepower." Races on ice, horses pulling skiers, were not uncommon. Oh boy, could we envision this sport!

There are two ways to skijor behind a horse. The first is using a specialized harness that attaches to the horse and from which a skier directs the horse as one skis behind. The second is pulling a skier behind a ridden horse. We, having subscribed to the "how hard could it be" school, tried both.

Two of us purchased from Holland the specialized harness from which we could ski behind our horses. The apparatus was much like a shopping cart handle on which the reins were attached by rods which, when moved, controlled the horse. The skier held onto the handle and controlled the horse through the rods. It seemed totally cool.

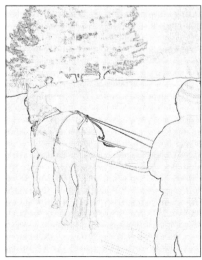

We took two very tolerant horses (who earned gold stars that day) and ventured out from our farm. The horses pulled us along via the handle, and we were having the best of times until we started downhill. Only then did it occur to us that Holland is flat. No one had factored hills into the design, and, as my skis slid forward into the trotting hind feet of my horse, I knew no good was going to come from this.

Through Herculean effort, I stopped my body from tumbling under my horse, but I was still unable to control the path of my skis. Shear dumb luck had them skimming along between his hind legs and they were now skimming along at a pretty good clip. I had not been paying too much attention to the control rods. The rods, I soon discovered, were at maximum tilt, which meant I had no control as long as we were traveling downhill. My skijoring partner, only a few feet behind me and gaining fast, was experiencing the same thing.

Had it not been for the change of terrain to uphill we would have been a train wreck for sure. And that is how it went for three miles; downhill in a complete lack of control, uphill, then downhill again. Every time my skis slid between my horse's hind feet I marveled that he did not seem to notice. There was simply nothing I could do about it, as the apparatus was able to stop my torso, but not my feet. Slack in the reins allowed the horses to plummet down the hills like a roller coaster, my friend and I the hapless passengers, silently screaming. The uphills allowed for regrouping, only to be followed by another plunge downward.

The final ascent up our farm's driveway was the last time I attempted such a tomfoolery. I sold the device to a person who assured me that he had a very flat place to try it out.

The second form of skijoring is to have a skier pulled by a rope that is attached to a ridden horse. This seemed a bit more sane until we attended a competition, a qualifying event, for the National Skijoring Championship held in Montana. Who knew such a thing existed?

Our friends were entered in the amateur class, and we braved February weather to see them compete. The course consisted of two ski jumps, four feet high, over which the skier had to jump. In order to gain points during the run, the rider had to skewer two sets of rings, while at a gallop, on either side before the jump. The zigzag pattern of the run produced acceleration of the skier whose speed had to be matched by the horse. I was thinking that my friends were nuts.

The first run showed us what happened when the horse was too slow. Having torqued up the skier by way of trajectory through the zigzag pattern, it was possible for the skier to arrive at the top of the jump before the horse. In such a case, the skier was left standing at the top as the horse raced past, rope tightening and the skier launched off of the jump like a slingshot. Some, in fact, landed cleanly and continued on. Amazing.

The bullet-like runs that produced clean jumps and good scores were, indeed, admirable to watch. Our friends managed to qualify for the amateur finals, but not without spending some time on the learning curve of the sport.

How to pull the skier seemed to come in many forms. Some folk just dallied a rope around the horn of a Western saddle, and others rigged a breast collar device. My friends, being carriage drivers, put on the breastplate of their harness and ran it back to a rope. Their mistake was that they ran the traces under the stirrups of the saddle.

Their horse was fast. Being a big-boned driving horse, she had no trouble launching herself out of the starting box and running with everything she had. Her rider started to notice a glitch in their plan when the skier swung left to get the first ring. As the trace pulled left, it lifted her leg, pitching her precariously into her right stirrup. The horse con-

tinued to run hard as the skier swung right, dropping her back into the saddle only to have the opposite trace lift her up into her left stirrup. The horse kept running. The rider experienced two more lifts. The skier had no idea that, miraculously, he was not attached to a running, riderless horse. They qualified, but they changed the rigging.

We eventually settled on a friendly, no longer hair raising, form of skijoring that placed a skier behind a mounted horse going UPHILL only. Visualize a type of water skiing on frozen water. We had learned, after the first skijoring adventure, that the shorter the skis, the better; less to tangle with hind feet, thank you very much. Skiing behind a galloping horse is, indeed, one of the best treats Vermont winters have to offer.

No Guilt, No Remorse

When you look a ferret straight in the eye, it is impossible to know what he is thinking. That stare down their nose reveals nothing. No guilt, no remorse, and no chance they are going to say, "I'm sorry." Whoever wrote *Ferrets Make Excellent Pets* made that plain with their repeated warnings about letting the ferret out of your sight. To have the run of the house was not suggested, in fact, strongly warned against. The book proposes toys and tunnels and ferret games to keep them happy. The reality is, however, that all a ferret really needs to be happy is a house. Just beware the consequences.

This jewel of knowledge was passed on to friends who were "baby sitting" a young ferret for their son's roommate over Thanksgiving vacation. They had met our Mr. Magoo and were enthralled with the idea of trying out a ferret for a week. A trial run, so to speak, for future plans. Their main concern was the dog. It took a few minutes of conversation before they realized that it would be the dog that needed protection. "They attack vacuum cleaners," I reminded them, "so what is a dog."

After careful inspection of their house, my friends completed the "look for where a ferret could get into trouble" search, and felt confident that at least two rooms would be ferret-safe. The ferret immediately proved them wrong by squeezing into a heat vent from which she toured the house. Two sleepless days and nights followed where they frantically followed the sounds of ferret footbeats through the walls, sometimes sleeping with their heads propped against the spot where sounds were last heard until awakened by the next rash of tiny footfalls. The prospect of rescue seemed impossible when the ferret finally popped her head out of a wall vent for a "look see" and they caught her. Whew.

Ferrets Make Excellent Pets was not kidding about how much trouble a free-range ferret could be! We know from first hand experience.

Mr. Magoo could have taught that ferret a thing or two about how to play with a house. First, it is a big toy so pacing oneself is crucial. Running helter skelter around a room is fine at first, but serious play needs thoughtful planning. Scouting for places to nap is very important. Places to nap are rated by their difficulty from which one can be retrieved. Under the gas stove and behind the TV are top rated locations. Boots are very attractive, but too often used by humans to be reliable.

Laundry hampers are lovely spots, but disruptive when one is being shaken out of a sound nap into a laundry basket. Closets are good, but contents change too often to offer a reliable place for a nap. Odd as it may seem, a plastic Igloo cooler provides ideal napping conditions when the weather is warm. This is based on ferret logic, not mine.

Basements are the Disney World of Ferrets. While it is hard to notice a change in a ferret's expression, clearly the discovery of the basement is a reason for joy. Half way down the cellar steps the ferret is bound to stop, look around, taking it all in, before continuing the decent at warp speed. At least one gallop around the basement is required before digging into the millions of hidey-holes begging for exploration. One has to be quick to see that expression of joy, but it certainly is there.

According to Webster – Toy; an object regarded as providing amusement. In ferret-speak, that is about everything. New object = new toy; something to remember when living with a ferret. The husband, although well schooled in the fine points of living with a free-range ferret, became the student of this lesson. Packing for a trip, he was famous for piling things on the "ferret-proof" table by the door so he would not forget them; a book to read, directions to the hotel, an umbrella (remember, the husband is English), the cell phone in a brand new leather case.

Only upon arriving at the airport would he discover he was the missing cell phone. A frantic search of his bags revealed nothing. The eventual call home had me search the table and surrounding area, nothing. The car was crawled over in detail when he got home. Nothing. Finally, he strode to the bedroom, scooped Mr. Magoo out of his clothes hamper, disturbing his fine nap, and started an interrogation. As I said, it is impossible to tell what a ferret is thinking although I am sure he was thinking his nap was more important than this nonsense.

"What would a ferret want with a cell phone?" queried the husband.

"I think it was the case he was interested in," I replied in an effort to calm the husband.

"Then he should give me back the phone!"

That began the house search that lasted four days. Every possible ferret spot was canvassed for the cell phone.

"Did you look behind the video player?"

"How about the china cupboard?"

"Inside the couch?"

"What about the pot and pan cabinet?"

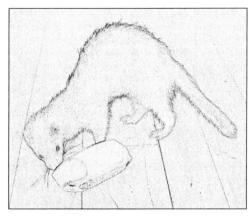

"He gets in there?"

"He can lie on his back and kick the door open."

"Is there no place that ferret doesn't go?"

No one was mentioning the basement. It would take a thousand years to search out every hidey-hole down there. I was fairly certain that I would have heard the thunkedty-thunk of a cell phone being dragged down a flight of cellar steps; but perhaps not. If it were in the basement, it might as well be in the black hole of Calcutta.

The husband finally gave up and called to report the cell phone missing. The amiable lady that takes care of such things inquired if the phone might have been stolen. "No," said the husband, "it is simply missing. Our ferret took it."

"Oh," she said, smart enough not to pursue that line of questioning. We got a new cell phone.

Two weeks later our "lost" phone showed up in the middle of the bedroom floor.

"How nice," I said, "he returned it."

No doubt, the husband felt a bit betrayed by the little weasel that lived with us. After all, the husband conceded his closet as a nap site, and put up with items being dragged under the gas stove from time to time. Their relationship had, in fact, bloomed to the point of showering together. Should he hear water running, Mr. Magoo would scratch incessantly on the door until he was scooped up and doused under the stream of water. The husband would flip him over, getting his belly side, before soaping him up for a vigorous scrub and then rinsing him off. Mr. Magoo loved his shower, which was reflected by his rolling and running and rolling and running all about the bathroom after being released. That kind of bonding should have precluded thievery and deceit, but apparently not.

One would think that the husband had learned his lesson but just a short time later his wallet went missing. Considerably more a loss than the cell phone, the searching and plotting of when and where it was last seen was immediate. To be sure, Mr. Magoo was not far from the husband's mind from the very beginning.

"Did you look behind the video player?"

"How about the china cupboard?"

"Inside the couch?"

"What about the pot and pan cabinet?"

"This time I am taking the entire couch apart."

Nothing. Mr. Magoo was taken in for interrogation, but that expressionless face showed no guilt, no remorse, and certainly no hint of where he stashed the wallet. I was on the little guy's side, after all, the husband should have learned from the cell phone.

"Where do you normally leave it?" I asked, thinking that perhaps a bit more care with one's personal objects was needed.

"Where I always leave it," responded the husband sternly, sure that he was within his rights to leave personal objects high on a "ferret proof" table. Until recently. Until we recently added a kitten to the household. Hmmm.

No doubt the kitten was working for Mr. Magoo.

The husband sighed, and started the series of phone calls one makes having lost a wallet. This time, between personal identity theft and homeland security, it was a bit harder to keep the credit card people from hitting red alert.

"No," explained the husband to the nice lady on the phone, "I don't think we have to cancel the credit cards, our ferret took the wallet."

"Yes, I am quite sure, he took the cell phone just last month."

"How do I know for sure? It showed up two weeks later."

"No, I don't know what he does with them, he just likes to hide things."

"Yes, he is very cute when he does things like that."

"No, he has never charged anything on the card."

The credit card lady had a sense of humor! As did the lady at the motor vehicle office who thought the story was hilarious, but the husband was still a bit annoyed about the whole experience.

Two weeks later the wallet showed up in the middle of the kitchen floor with all of the money intact.

"A ferret is God's way of telling you NOTHING is childproof."

IN QUEST OF A WHITE PONY

Have you ever seen a white pony? I mean white! I have a barn full of almost white ponies, but never once, even for a split second, have I seen one that was truly white, or wanted to be. The truth is that white ponies are not happy being white. Any other color seems to suit – brown, green, blue, pink, anything but white. Some get very artistic, and could pass themselves off as pintos or palominos any day of the week.

The root of the problem is that they all start out as brown, bay, or black. The introduction of gray hair starts shortly after weaning; by yearlings the telltale white hairs let you know that, year by year, this bay foal will eventually change out to be white. By the time the pony is half grown, the white hairs will have outnumbered the dark and we call them rose greys, dapple greys, flea bitten greys, or just grey. The important thing to remember is that grey is half way to white.

By the time you or your child have fallen madly in love with the grey, soon to be white, pony, it is too late. Every year the pony will win some blue ribbons and every year the pony will get more white hairs until one morning, you open up the stall door and there, where your grey pony once stood, is a pure as the driven snow, sparkling in the sunshine, white pony. "Oh, he's so beautiful," you mutter until you notice the large manure stain the shape of Long Island on his belly. Welcome to the elite membership of "almost white ponies."

When the pony was still grey, you had it made. An even mixture of dark and white hair is the perfect color not to show dirt. As he lightened, girth stains were explained as "roan spots" in his coat. Fence rubs were varnish marks, and dust was dapples. The party is over when they turn white. White is White!

The first thing you have to do is color test all of your equipment. Never trust a green tail wrap, never use a new halter and never, ever put a red sheet on a clean, wet white pony. Never buy a new bridle, girth, or harness, and just plop it on the pony. Never use latigo leather, dyed leather or harness black. And never, ever, turn your pony out where the fence is treated with black preservatives.

When a show rolls around, the real challenge is not only to get the pony white, but also to keep him white until he gets into the ring. After that, the show is a cinch. It starts two days ahead with the "preliminary bath and clip". This is to remove all the ground in dirt and, hopefully, clip off some of the tinged brown hair. The pony is moved to a "clean place", which means he can get only half as dirty as where he is usually kept. The next day is the "real bath," the one with the bluing, special shampoos and scrub brushes. The pony is washed three times, the first for  dirt, the second for dirt that did not come out the first time, and the third in hopes that it will come out this time. When every product used has failed to get out the yellow stain on his left leg, you decide to tell everyone that his mother was a pinto.

Now comes the hard part. What do you do with a clean, white pony? Sitting up with him all night or wrapping him in cellophane may cross your mind. Instead, you put him in a clean stall, wearing his color tested sheet and plan to rise two hours earlier than everyone else with a bay pony just in case he may need another bath in the morning. You toss and turn all night with white ponies dancing through your nightmares.

The next challenge is the horse trailer, scrubbed down in preparation for the clean, white pony, you load up and hope for the best. Arriving an hour earlier than everyone else, you unload and strip off the sheet and bandages. Only four spots! Anyone arriving at a show with a clean, white pony should immediately be presented with a blue ribbon!

The tack or harness goes on and you make it to the show ring. Your magnificent white pony, gleaming in the early morning sun, almost blinds those that come to admire him.

"Who's this?" your neighbor asks.

"Why, it's Dapples, of course!"

"Dapples? I thought he was a palomino?"

"Ha ha." Let them laugh, but you have the whitest of white ponies there and catch everyone's eye. It was all worth it in the end, for you get the blue ribbon and trot off to your trailer. While removing the tack you suddenly see a long brown stain where the rein touched his neck. Oh, no! Quickly, you grab some suds and start scrubbing, determined not to let the stain set in and cursing your tack shop for not getting the special leather you requested.

The bottom line about white ponies is that no matter now dirty they get, or how many extra hours you spend getting them white, they are worth it. Just mention to the pony club leader that you have a white pony to get ready for a show and you can get out of anything. Have a friend complain about his horse's white socks and your white pony will shut him up; pronto. When white ponies are white, their flowing white tails and their gleaming white coats set them apart from every other color, even the greys. Just give them a little more time....

WHAT A DEY!

Distance riding can be a tough sport. Riding for hours in the rain. Riding for hours in the heat. Sleeping in the back of a horse trailer with your horse tied outside; not getting much sleep with your horse bumping the trailer all night. But for all true distance riders, such little things are not about to stand in their way of having fun. Marie Dey was no exception.

Marie rode her first distance ride with the reins in one hand and the rulebook in the other. That first ride in 1972 got her hooked, and she had become a fixture in the sport by the time I started competing. Marie had not entered into distance riding very gracefully. There was that time that Fran Grant's horse, Patton, broadsided her horse, dumping Marie in a most embarrassing position to the ground. Marie was toted across the finish line in a like-fashion as a sheriff would bring in a dead outlaw. Still, she won the ride.

Such was Marie's luck. Her two horses, Timber and Diamond, brought home enough loot to fill the house, the barn and the garage. All of these awards had brought her to the attention of the press, in which one article applauded her for being "one of the best elder riders in the State." Marie's comment was, "Thanks for pointing that out!"

One would think that, with all of those miles, Marie would have acquired the directional senses of an Indian. Sorry to say she was often the first to get lost, even when someone else pointed out the right way. She expanded this ability, or lack of, to the thruways, where she had been known to speed right past an exit, despite the frantic gestures of her companions.

Not one to sit at home when she was not competing, Marie volunteered to head up the veterinary team for driving events. I was always happy to see that familiar face when I drove my ponies into the vet box, for I knew that all was under control. Likewise, Marie always greeted me with a wide grin and personally saw to my needs. All was well until I decided to try combined driving with a tandem. I could see by Marie's expression that she thought I was nuts.

The husband's tandem, which was considerably difficult to drive, gave Marie's nerves a run through while they were at the hold. She had barely recovered when I arrived. Gingerly, she placed the thermometer into the leader, and turned her attention to expressing her genuine concern for my welfare. Mid-sentence, she was summoned by a very distraught crew member. "I can't find the thermometer!" Every horse-man knows that losing a horse thermometer is serious business, but with the calm that comes with years of experience, Marie turned an ac-cusing eye on my wheeler just in time to pluck the missing thermom-eter from her inquisitive little lips. Now, whenever Marie instructs a veterinary team, she clearly points out that it is inadvisable to leave a leader's thermometer unattended as wheelers cannot be trusted.

Marie was so busy riding, judging and volunteering, that find-ing her at home was harder than keeping track of thermometers. Her answering machine message was suited just right for Marie. "Hello, you have reached stall #6. The mare isn't in right now, but come along feeding time, she'll be home and call you right back." And she did.

My most memorable experience with Marie was at our riding club's award dinner. The elaborate program of entertainment in-cluded "Mazie, the Amazing Horse", a vaudeville horse costume that winked, blinked, wiggled, wagged and whinnied. A nationwide talent search had selected the two best suited people to bring "Mazie" to life. Marie was unanimously chosen, along with another well known whifty distance rider, Debbie. Behind closed doors, they giggled and wiggled into the costume while they played with the frayed nerves of the skit co-ordinator who tried in vain to get them to rehearse their lines.

We were all happily gob-bling up our desserts when the band struck up a trumpet call to bring us all to attention. Dressed in a flowing gown, reminiscent of a 1940's movie, the lady of cer-emony announced the arrival of "Mazie, the Amazing Horse." Marie and Debbie wasted no time by racing into the banquet hall at a full "gallop", sliding "gracefully" into an awaiting chair. I could see the skit coordinator cringing by the door. The skit was to reenact the vetting procedure that all riders are so familiar with at com-petitions. What "Mazie" did not know, because she was too busy gig-gling to pay attention to the skit coordinator, was that the thermometer was three feet long and that the vet was an unsuspecting soul chosen from the audience.

At the sight of the thermometer, "Mazie" went from a quiet, lovely, little mare, to a wild, striking mustang. Every attempt to raise her tail resulted in the vet being sat on, stepped on and backed over. In reality, we all remarked that such things do happen at rides! The sad result was that "Mazie's" tail came off into the veterinarian's hand. We all agreed that we'd never seen that happen before!

The audience was becoming "Mazie's". Sensing that, the old mare played to the crowd, leaving the vet, the cast and the poor skit coordinator to do their best to follow her. Proving, once again, that horses are superior to human beings, "Mazie" took her bow and left under a thunder of applause.

Still giggling, Marie and Debbie rejoined the banquet festivities, but this time dressed as "people". Everyone was anxious to congratulate them on a brilliant performance, and, of course, anxious to find out just who was which end of the horse. To this day, when put to this question, Marie will answer, "I'm not that much of a fool to admit that I was a horse's behind!"

THE YARDSTICK

Early in my endurance riding career I could be talked into doing just about anything. I no longer buy into the "it will be fun" thing because I know better. However, such experiences are memorable and provide a yardstick in which to measure all future forms of discomfort one might encounter while out riding in the great outdoors. This particular weekend has yet to be beat.

Having just moved to Vermont we were still a bit naïve about October. In Pennsylvania it was considered a fall foliage month, one with warms days and brisk nights and perhaps the first frost. In Vermont, it was the month one prepares for winter as it could show up at any minute.

My friend, Heather, talked me into taking our horses to the Blue Ridge Mountains in Virginia for a three day, one hundred and fifty mile ride. "It will be fun." Heather was not a complete fool for she was riding only two days. I would crew for her on the first and ride the second. It did sound like fun.

Twelve hours later we arrived in camp with Heather's trailer which was bare bones but very adequate for fair weather camping. It had a nice bed over the gooseneck part of the trailer and a makeshift "kitchen" consisting of a propane camp stove and a water jug. We had an awning for Heather's horse and a tarp which we tied high to trees for mine. My Morgan was a bit hesitant about that arrangement when it flapped so he stood as far out in his pen as possible. All in all we had a neat little camp going, and after vetting in our horses joined the rest of the riders at the campfire.

It had been quite warm. The hardy group who had ridden that day was still in T-shirts and welcomed the forecast of some cooler weather moving in for the weekend. Possible rain in the morning, with increased probability throughout the day, was the forecast. However, north of us, up in Vermont, a nasty storm was brewing with plummeting temps, and perhaps the first snow of the season. "Ha", we said, snug in warm Virginia, "too bad for them."

Indeed, the next day started out perfectly for riding as fifty-some riders left camp in the pre-dawn, leaving off sparks as the horses' hooves struck down the trail. I made sure my horse was happy in his encampment before heading out to help Heather at the two scheduled vet stops along the trail during the day. I threw a light jacket and raincoat into the truck, just in case. I so was deliriously happy about being in the Virginia sunshine, rather than back in Vermont where it was snowing that I did not, but should have, checked with the weatherman.

By the first stop on the trail, it was clear that the cooler weather was getting cooler and cooler. By the second stop, it was downright cold. Fifty miles takes about eight to ten hours to ride, including stops, and in that period of time the weather took us from Indian summer to the brink of winter. "At least it isn't raining," someone said.

Riders who had started the day with light clothing were begging for anything anyone could spare. One rider put a spare set of panties on her head, under her helmet, to help her stay warm. Heather fared a bit better, thanks to my last minute addition of the jacket and raincoat, but that left me with a single towel as a "cloak." With the heat on full blast, I drove her Ford truck over the course to the next stop. The finish line was a welcomed sight for everyone. Once through the vet checkpoint, the horses were bundled into blankets, and riders scrambled to find more warm clothing. That evening, the campfire looked a lot more like a Christmas scene than the evening before. "At least it isn't raining," someone said. The first drop fell with an ominous "hiss" into the fire and was followed by a host more.

There is not much more to do on a cold, rainy night in an endurance camp than go to bed. We had turned Heather's Ford truck into a clothes dryer after our mad scramble for the trailer and securing camp soaked us. The tarp had taken on a life of its own: filling with runoff water to the point where it would flip, and dump, several gallons at a time, in whatever direction it chose. One unhappy Morgan was standing under the tarp with his ears pinned in order to show his delight in his situation. He managed to find the only safe spot and, to his credit, remained there all night. He was not happy, but at least he was dry.

NO VEHICLES BEYOND THIS POINT

I wish I could say the same for us. The Ford was doing its best as a dryer, but our sopping wet boots were beyond its ability; we did not have spares. By flashlight, we sorted through our gear and managed to put together a reasonably weatherproof outfit for the next day. We yanked the carrots out of their bags and used the bags as "socks." Heather dug into her jacket pockets and produced several pairs of gloves. I had the foresight to pack an extra sweatshirt. Did it occur to us not to ride? NO. Did it occur to us that eight to ten hours of rain might be more than our gear could handle? NO. Did it occur to us that we were nuts? Of course not, "it will be fun."

The pounding of rain greeted us as we struggled to get all of our clothes on and tack up our horses in the dark. Endurance rides very often start in the dark so that no one misses one minute of daylight. Twelve hours of daylight is hard to come by in late October; daylight on a cold rainy day is even harder to find. But we all saddled up and started down the trail, optimism our co-pilot, thinking, "it will be fun."

The trails in the Blue Mountains of Virginia are pretty spectacular. There are vistas overlooking the Shenandoah River that are breathtaking. Some of the high ridge trails were traveled as supply routes for the troops by Civil War soldiers. However spectacular, they are also extremely rocky and steep. Very rocky. Very steep. There was no view that day, nor would I see that view for twelve more years until I finally rode a ride in Virginia that did not have rain or fog.

There was no problem traveling with speed in the valley. By the time dawn had broken, more than half of the horses were miles ahead of me. I had chosen a slower pace for my Morgan who did not yet have the experience to go faster. I had plenty of company, as many riders were also taking care in the inclement weather. We had not seen much of the first eight miles of the course between the darkness and the rain. Heather, on her good horse, Revy, was long gone. I had the excitement of riding to keep me warm and all in all, it didn't seem so bad.

My first indication that the day might not turn out as hoped was passing a road sign that said "Winter Road Maintenance Ends Here". That was followed shortly by a sign that said "Four Wheel Drive Vehicles Only," and then "No Vehicles Beyond this Point." No doubt, we were headed up a ridge, a steep, rocky, twisting trail up a ridge. No choice but to walk. Up and up, over the rocks, up and up, more rocks, to the top, finally, then down and down, over the rocks, down and down, more rocks.

About three quarters of the way up that first hill I felt the first trickle of rain sneak its way down my back. I was soon to discover that any rain gear, proclaiming to be water repellant, had a time limit. To this day, short of a garbage bag, I have never found a garment that will keep me dry on a horse. The garbage bag did not work that great either. I did all the adjustments I could but could not keep that drip from being followed by others. By the time I got off of that ridge not only was I wet, I was cold.

Greeting me at the bottom was the first vet check, forty minutes during which the vets examined my horse and we got to eat and pee. I could not wait. The Morgan, honoring his breed, showed no signs of wear and tear and trotted briskly for the vets so that they could see this. Never mind my Herculean effort to keep up with him. He dove into his food and was just as happy as could be for a horse standing in an open field on a cold, rainy day. I, on the other hand, had to pee really badly and wanted desperately to adjust some wet clothing, particularly that next to my skin.

I snagged a nice lady to hold onto my horse while I trudged up the hill to the porta potty with almost unbearable anticipation for getting to my undergarments. My hand had just reached for the door when a ruckus went up at the timer station. "Stop, stop!" they yelled, "stop that horse!" I looked over with that gut feeling that the horse, the one dragging a nice lady, would be mine. Sure enough, the Morgan had decided he was done with the hold and was taking to the trail, lady in tow. Only thanks to the timers did that lady not see the rest of the course.

Springing, as much as anyone wearing forty pounds of wet clothing could spring, I rescued the nice lady, and apologized profusely to the timers. They did not look too amused. My Morgan did not appear to show one bit of remorse and was still looking down the trail. My bladder whimpered and, in desperation, I hollered out to the crew area, "Anyone here tough enough to hold this Morgan so I can pee?" Endurance riders are one incredible class of people. A gal strode up, grabbed that Morgan, and had him standing at attention when I returned from my ever so pleasant, but short, time in that porta potty. Whoever you were, thank you!

Time flies at a vet check, and I was too soon on my horse and back on the trail. I did feel a bit better, clothing adjustment wise, and the valley trail offered some decent riding that warmed me up considerably. My horse was perky and felt terrific under me and, despite the increasing rain, it was not that bad.

Then the road signs started again. "Winter Road Maintenance Ends Here", "Four Wheel Drive Vehicles Only," and finally "No Vehicles Beyond this Point." By the time we started the climb up the next ridge I was joined by several riders, one of whom was very experienced. I was rather flattered to be riding with her, while at the same time wondering why she was riding in the back of the ride.

"What a dreadful day," she muttered in her smooth Southern accent, adjusting her rain gear in what we both knew to be a futile effort to stay dry. "Just look on over there," she quipped as we spotted some hardy campers in a tent, "why who be out here on a day like this when ya'll don't have to be?" They waved back to us, smiling, perhaps laughing, as we certainly did not look anywhere as good as they did.

"Don't you think they think the same of us?" I replied.

"Not at all," came the experienced answer, "we paid to do this." It then struck me, indeed, that we had in fact paid for this pleasure.

As we rose up the ridge the rain seemed to drop off, certainly a welcome measure, until we realized that it had turned to snow. The rocky trail was more than a bit slippery and the horses poked along the best they could. As we breached Sherman's gap, I could hear one of the group whimpering; she was so cold. Our experienced comrade showed no mercy, "Shush, it's not that bad." But it was. I had given my horse his head and was sitting on my hands, not that it helped much as my saddle was just as wet as I was. The snow stuck to our wet clothing giving us a ghostlike appearance as we arrived at the second, and last hold.

Since we were the back of the ride, the volunteers and vets waiting for us were huddled next to a fire they had built to keep from freezing to death while waiting for us. We were told, in a most matter of fact way, that we should hurry things up a bit. None of us were able to get off of our horses as our feet were so numb. The vet told us just to trot out mounted, declared us looking fine and shouted, "pick up the pace!" as we left.

The rain was still falling in the valley and washed off our snow coat as we trundled along towards the finish. I had been riding for ten hours, had eaten nothing, drank nothing, peed only once and could feel only parts of my body. The Morgan, on the other hand, had gobbled down everything he was fed, peed four times, drank like a fish, and was thinking this was all pretty much fun. This would be an omen for the next twenty years during which I competed this incredible horse, and a sure sign that I was going to have to get a lot tougher to survive it.

When I dismounted at the finish, checking to see if my numb feet were, indeed on the ground, Heather, who had finished hours earlier, greeted me. "Hey, great to see you," which meant, "where have you been all day?" The Morgan demonstrated to the vets that he was hardly stressed from the day's ordeals, and we received one of the hardest earned completions of my career.

All I wanted to do at that point was get out of those wet clothes! With the added mud and wet, I had about fifty pounds dragging me down as I plodded towards our camp.   Heather fired up the Ford and had it blowing balmy, warm air out of the heater as I crawled in to strip down. Helmet, raincoat, jacket, sweatshirt, turtleneck, second turtleneck, T- shirt, all soaked. Half-chaps, boots, socks, second socks, pants, all soaked. No underwear. The underwear had been left in that first porta potty.

As I pulled on the last dry clothes I owned, I tuned on the radio. "A freak winter storm came out of nowhere today and hit the entire Eastern seaboard," the announcer, sitting in his nice, dry, warm studio, was saying. "Cold air from Canada broke through a front and poured down on the wet air coming up from Georgia, causing snow to break out at the higher elevations of the Blue Ridge Mountains in Virginia to the Appalachian Mountains in Maine," No kidding, I knew that. "The situation will worsen, and up to a foot of snow can be expected overnight."

"What!!!"

Bolting out of the truck, I grabbed Heather and told her the "good" news. Two other riders, having just heard the same thing, started frantically throwing their gear into their truck. In fact, the entire camp started moving for the road. We had little choice, other than to spend the night and perhaps the next week in an unheated trailer with two horses tied to trees, than to make a dash for it.

No time. We grabbed all of our wet gear, saddles, bridles, horse blankets, riding clothes, boots, underwear, and tossed them into the front of the trailer. I grabbed both horses to hold while Heather gunned up her Ford and, sending rooster tails of mud flying fifteen feet over the trailer roof, drove through the waterlogged camp grounds, around two hulking trees, had a close miss with another trailer to arrive safely on the firm gravel road out of there. That was some impressive driving!

As we trailered up Edinburgh Gap, altitude twenty-five hundred feet, the weatherman, all excited about this renegade snowstorm, announced, "Anyone camping in the Blue Ridge Mountains is being evacuated as the potential snowfall could have the Gap closed for days." Heather gunned up the Ford some more.

Back home, in Vermont, the husband was getting the full force of the storm. Over a foot had fallen and more was predicted. He had scrambled to get the chains on the tractor but thought he was in good shape. "Wow, this is some welcome to Vermont," he said.

"Honey, I replied, I'm in Virginia and we are getting snow."

"Really?"

"Really."

"Well, you can't come home, the roads are awful."

Gee, just want I wanted to hear. I was still cold, despite the Ford's efforts, I had no dry clothes, and more than anything I wanted a long, hot shower. Even driving twelve hours to get one seemed reasonable. I could see that this day was not over yet.

Heather and I put our heads together for any friends we had who lived somewhere between Virginia and Vermont, where we could hole up for a day or two. Having two horses along narrowed down our choices. One heartwarming thing about being a horse owner is that you get to know many decent people who are willing to take you in when in a state of destitution. Thankfully, we knew someone only a few hours away. Heather pointed her Ford to Pennsylvania.

Even though the snow had caught up with us, we had enough time to secure the horses in a pleasant barn and get to our friend's house before midnight when the real storm hit. There had been no time for eating other than grabbing whatever food forms there are at a fuel station. We were dog-tired when we headed for bed, but first there was no question that we had to take a shower. Who would go first? Heather had performed so admirably well getting us out of Virginia I offered her that privilege. "Thank you," she said as she bolted for the door. Then she paused, turned back to me and said, "If I am not back in fifteen minutes, I have fallen asleep in the shower and you should come rescue me."

"Got it," I said.

There is no better feeling, nothing, than a hot shower after riding fifty or one-hundred miles. I often think that riders do this silly sport just for the feeling of that shower. No other shower feels the same. The water spreads over your body with warming hands, it hits your feet like a massage, and it runs down your back like a warm kitten. One just stands with eyes closed and feels the shower, perhaps for ten minutes, before soaping up and doing damage control on the body. It is just the best feeling, ever. Heather and I still remember that one.

Two days later, when the roads finally cleared, we arrived home in Vermont. There was no point unloading our gear, it was frozen solid into a massive pile; it remained there until spring. The winter storm was talked about for a week by the weatherman who, never once, apologized for missing that call. Both Heather and I use that ride as the yardstick by which we measured all other rides.

"Was it worse than that time in Virginia?" she would ask after I came home from a particularly weather nasty weekend.

"No," I admitted.

"Then it wasn't so bad!"

Aren't You the Same Kid ...?

B usy working with a two year old filly, I did not notice the young man walk into the barn. The horse was being fussy about having her bridle adjusted and needed my attention. Finally she relaxed, and I turned to greet my guest.

"May I speak with the owner of the stable please," he asked in a practiced manner.

"I am the owner," I replied, "how may I help you?"

Unnerved by getting the head person right off, he cleared his throat several times before speaking. "I would like to work for you on weekends," he said nervously, "and over the summer if you need help."

Before I could answer, my horse started to fuss again and I had to excuse myself. My young guest watched with interest as I gently rubbed the filly's face and turned her so she could see the other horses through the window. When I resumed the conversation, I spied our current young stable lad doing his best to listen in from the nearby tack room. He was all ears.

"Do you know anything about horses?" I queried.

"Oh, yes, ma'am," my guest proudly stated. "My neighbor used to have one."

I heard a cough from the tack room.

"Do you know how to groom a horse?"

Nervously eying my filly, who was again starting to fuss, he replied, "No, but I can learn."

Another cough.

I smiled, "Of course, and we would be happy to teach you if you worked here."

Relieved that I was not going to make him demonstrate his skill on my poorly acting filly, he returned my smile. In that smile, I saw generations of young faces who all started their careers with horses by making that first significant contact: someone with a barn full of horses and the patience to teach. That foundation would serve them for the rest of their lives as horsemen.

He left his phone number and would be coming to work over the upcoming school vacation. He headed home with a smile and keen anticipation of learning whatever one needs to know to work in a horse barn. I could tell that the "horse bug" had bitten and that he could not wait to be part of all of this.

I gave the filly a reprimand and reminded her that she had better manners than what she had recently displayed. My trip to the tack room had me just about fall over the eavesdropping P.J.

Unable to contain himself, he handed down his opinion, "He won't last."

"Who?"

"That kid, that's who."

"Why not? He seems very interested."

P.J. looked at me with exasperation. "You will have to teach him everything," he retorted. "He doesn't even know how to groom a horse!"

With that, he stepped out into the aisle and deftly tapped my filly on the shoulder to distract her from pawing. I watched him talk to her softly and adjust her bridle so it was perfect in its fit. He then swung a saddle up over her back, allowing it to land lightly in order not to frighten her. He pulled up the girth gently and continued to adjust her tack until he was satisfied.

"Wait a minute," I said, trying to regain my authority. "Aren't you the same kid who showed up here with that same request just a few years ago?"

That kid, now a handsome, six-foot tall equestrian, was only too eager not to be reminded that he was once a green horn. He started to squirm.

"Yes," I continued, "I do remember that you had that same look. Aren't you the same kid that filled all the feed troughs with water? The same kid who could not tell a bay from a chestnut for the longest time? The kid who keep putting the bit on the bridle backwards? The very same kid who did not get out of a walk for almost a month when we taught you to ride?"

"Okay, okay!" he protested. "But I learned, didn't I?"

"Exactly my point."

He started to say something, then decided to let one of his disarming grins be his response. I knew then that the new kid would have an outstanding teacher.

SUNDAY BREAKFAST

The decision to hook the horses to a brimming full manure spreader on that cold, and fateful day in January was not one that Bob made without due consideration. Bob, the engineer, thought through all tasks with resolute care. There were times during which just changing his shoes took time consuming deliberation. However, on this particular day, Bob found himself in the predicament of miscalculation.

The horses, it turns out, had not held to the estimated amount of manure Bob had intended to muck from their stalls that week. Perhaps it was that extra flake of hay one evening or it could have been as simple as too many carrots; the fact remained that the manure runneth over.

Bob could not ignore this as his coworkers had started commenting on the specific odor of his clothing and joking, "Hey Bob, do you live in a barn?" The fact was that Bob did live in his barn along with four quite large Percheron horses. It was a temporary situation made necessary by one of the few impulsive acts of his otherwise well ordered life. Upon receiving his final divorce papers, Bob bought a motorcycle and headed West. When he got to Indiana, he discovered the Topeka Draft Horse and Livestock Auction. Bob, a horse neophyte, was so enamored by what he saw, he sold the motorcycle, bought a truck and trailer, and sat down to bid on a pair of black Percherons. They were almost last in the sale order and Bob, the engineer, started to worry about being outbid, and have no horses at all. That was when he bought the two greys. And of course, the pair of blacks.

By the time Bob purchased some harness and a forecart, he had just enough funds to drive to Pennsylvania. Living in the barn with his horses allowed him to have enough money to buy a car and eat until he recovered financially. It was a quite cozy, tack room with Dutch doors that allowed two of the horses to stick their heads in while Bob made dinner. Bob kept the barn meticulously clean until a particularly cold and nasty week of weather necessitated keeping the horses in their stalls all day and all night.

The horse manure was carted from the stalls and dumped into an old, but very functional, horse drawn manure spreader. Bob, the engineer, saw no need for a tractor when he had four horsepower of horses. Once a week Bob would hitch up two horses to the spreader and empty it over a five-acre hay field. The miscalculation became obvious by Thursday evening and little could be done to convince the horses that they were headed towards maximum capacity in the stalls. They blithely produced more manure.

Bob, the engineer, calculated that, by Saturday morning, he would reach terminal mass and planned to spread that day. But Mother Nature could not help but add to the situation by dropping freezing rain. By Sunday morning, Bob revisited the situation and, appreciative of the possible complications, hitched Daisy and Dan, the blacks, to the manure spreader. Bob thought he had covered all of the possible scenarios and was prepared, as all engineers were, to adjust his plan accordingly.

The first adjustment came with the horses. Having been stalled most of the week, they had a bit more enthusiasm for the job than usual. Bob was thinking that the weight of the overloaded manure spreader would settle them down, so he took them far out into the field, out by the new houses, before engaging the gears of the spreader.

The manure was moved by two chains, which slid the load to spinning blades that threw the manure out of the spreader. The apparatus was driven by gears that were connected to the moving wheels. The horsepower was provided, naturally, by the horses. So, when the gears were engaged, more horsepower would be needed. On this particular cold winter day, the manure was frozen into one massive bulk. The horse power required to break that loose caused Daisy and Dan to lunge into the harness, and give it their all. Bob, the engineer, still failed to see the flaw in his plan.

Once the manure spreader became operational, the horses picked up speed. The faster they went, the more manure was thrown, the lighter the load, the faster they went, and the further the manure was thrown. Frozen solid, hard as a rock, missiles of manure bombarded the aluminum siding of the new houses. The machine gun like effect roused numerous families from their breakfast to peer flabbergasted out of their windows. Flying by was Bob, Daisy and Dan, galloping on a circular course around the field.

Bob, the engineer, remained calm, as he knew there was no such thing as a perpetual motion machine; eventually they would stop. He was calculating his speed and computing the lessening load of the spreader in order to arrive at that point. Had he consulted Daisy and Dan, he would have realized that he had forgotten to calculate in the fun factor. At each pass, the houses were bombarded; the breakfasters surely under their kitchen tables huddled in fear that one of the missiles would crash through a window. Bob thought about saying, "Oh, #*@!," but that would have been redundant as #*@! was flying everywhere.

Animal Lovers' Barometer

If you wake up with three dogs, two cats and a ferret in bed with you
     – it is cold outside

If your cat or dog is wet
     – it is raining

If your dog has stuffed itself behind the couch
     – there is a thunderstorm brewing.

If the cat is sleeping in the sink
     – it is hot

If your dog is fat
     – you are not getting enough exercise

If you wake up with a cat swatting your face
     – you have overslept, even if you don't think so.

Animal Lovers' Mantras

The cat is always right.

There are never too many horses in the barn.

The dog is smarter than most people.

I could have a private jet or have pets.

My mother would die if she saw this.

My children will be better people because of this.

Animal Lovers' Socially Correct Dinner Guest Guide

Always greet someone's pet as if you would a member of the family.

Include the pet in any house presents you bring.

Never ask how many pets someone has in front of their spouse.

Never, as a guest, sit in the pet's favorite chair.

If you do sit in the pet's favorite chair by accident, move, even if the hostess says its OK. It is not OK with the pet.

Never wear white clothing or black clothing to a house full of pets. Especially if the pet has a favorite chair.

Always ask to see the most recent pictures of a pet of they are not present.

Always ask to see the barn, horses and tack room, before dinner.

Never ask the non-horsey spouse to join you.

Do your best to talk about something other than an animal's last injury or illness during dinner.

Always bring up one subject not related to horses, pets or animals so you can lay claim to not monopolizing the dinner conversation with only those interests when driving home with your spouse.

Ignore all doggy odors and sounds during pre-dinner conversations.

Feel free to play footsie under the table with the host's dog or cat during dinner. Be sure it is the dog or cat.

Laugh about all the doggy odors and sounds after dinner.

Always ask the hostess about saving dinner scraps for pets when helping with the dishes.

Always leave with an open invitation to walk dogs, ride horses, or just hang out with pets at your house.

ABOUT THE AUTHOR

Sue Greenall grew up in suburban New Jersey and earned a B.S. in Animal Science from Rutgers University. She taught high school biology for ten years before marrying the husband. The Green Mountains of Vermont are home for their "Dr. Doolittle" environment of animals. A thirty-year old horse wanders free on the farm as does the goat and goose and the ferret is often seen peeking out from under the kitchen stove. The symmetry of the farm is reflected in the stories in the book. Sue has been a successful free-lance writer for many horse publications. She has two other books, *The Animal Lovers' Bedtime Reader* and *The Vermonters' Guide to Gathering Growing & Cooking with Local Foods*. She is also an accomplished horsewoman in carriage driving, competitive trail riding and endurance and has competed throughout the United States. She has a Tevis buckle and represented the USEF at two Pan American Endurance Championships. Her favorite pastimes are swimming in the pond, snowshoeing with the dogs and riding her horse in the moonlight.

ABOUT THE COVER ARTIST

It is no surprise that Beth Carlson's sporting art paintings and portraits are coveted by many animal lovers across the country. Her ability to constantly capture an individual animal's personality and physical characteristics can be directly attributed to her far-reaching knowledge pertaining to animals in general. The book cover and inside artwork have graced the cover of "The Chronicle of the Horse." Beth resides on the coast of Maine with her husband, fox hunter and two dogs.

Animal Lovers' Bedside Stories

All of my books have been written, formatted and edited by myself. Of course, the husband helped, as did some great friends who were willing to read over my manuscripts and offer welcome suggestions. I launched into my first book without knowing what I was doing and learned as I went. Many thanks to R.C. Brayshaw Printers for their help and support. Using a local printer was indeed a boon! The books have sold all over the United States thanks to the connections we have with the horse world. Animal shelters have used the book as a fund raiser and a school in South Carolina uses the stories in their reading program. I love that many of my readers have contacted me to share stories of their own. If you would like another copy or are interested in using books for fund raising, please contact me through one of these methods.

EASY ORDER

WWW.GREENALLCARRIAGE.COM
PAY PAL ACCEPTED

GREENALL@VERMONTEL.NET

Animal Lovers' Bedside Stories - $12.95

Animal Lovers' Bedtime Reader - $12.95

The Vermonters' Guide to $9.95
Gathering,
Growing
& Cooking with
Local Foods